GOOD NEWS

from
great
leaders

D1561854

Robert D. Dale

AN ALBAN INSTITUTE PUBLICATION

The Publications Program of The Alban Institute is assisted by a grant from
Trinity Church, New York City.

Library of Congress Catalog Card #91-78150.

CONTENTS

ACKNOWLEDGMENTS

Huge redwood trees grow from shallow root systems, according to horticulturists. How do they keep from being uprooted and blown over? They intertwine their roots with the nearby trees. That's a fitting metaphor for how the ideas for books are supported and gain their sturdiness too. Authors only produce books with the intertwining support of adjoining contributors.

Risking the chance that I will not name all the contributors in my network of influence for this book, I want to say thanks to several key support givers. Ernest Mosley, Howard Foshee, Randall Lolley, and Reggie McDonough have provided me the professional opportunity to specialize in the art and science of religious leadership for more than two decades. Several generations of conference participants, seminarians, and participants in the Young Leaders' Program of Virginia Baptists as well as Billy Davis and the Genesis class of Richmond's Derbyshire Baptist Church have helped shape the principles in this book. Luke Smith and Bob Perry helped evaluate the ideas in the manuscript. And, these persons and groups represent only the most obvious rootages for this material. Other advisors, writers, theorists, and practitioners have also contributed. I thank them all and appreciate their intertwining support. In spite of the fact that this book is rooted in their influences as the footnotes indicate, I hold none of them directly responsible for the ideas I've put forward in these pages.

INTRODUCTION

Good News from Great Leaders!

Leaders act. That's the bottom line. Leaders do things. At least, leaders *try* to do things—by influencing others and changing circumstances basically. When we lead, we have a ripple effect on the people around us and on the situations we operate in. Leaders act; followers react; the situation changes. That's what leaders do—that's leadership in its simplest form.

The actions of leaders are evident in the Bible. *Good News from Great Leaders*, a biblical and theological perspective on religious leadership, provides an overview of twenty key leadership incidents in the Bible, identification of leaders' actions, and practical applications for religious leaders today.

The Bible records many great leadership stories—a fact that's good news for contemporary leaders. I've selected only twenty of these key episodes, however, due to space considerations. Therefore, there's still more good news for your leadership development in other biblical episodes.

The Bible is viewed here more as a casebook on leadership than a codebook.[1] That is, the Bible is used here to describe a selective series of leadership examples reflecting a range of responses in a variety of circumstances. You and I are still left with the responsibility of reflecting on and interpreting the biblical examples as well as applying the leadership insights to our particular situations. In short, the Bible provides a rich array of instructive leadership vignettes without prescribing our specific actions

for us. The challenge of applying these biblical cases to our
leadership opportunities is straightforward: we need not only to
understand the Bible and human nature, but to know God. That's
the first foundation for religious leaders.

A Word from Our Sponsor: Action

Ultimately, God is the leader in the Bible. God has led redemptively through his "mighty acts."[2] His actions in creation, judgment, restoration, and salvation have shaped, and continue to
influence, history. Persons of faith have asserted that God is, by
nature and example, an initiative taker, a thoughtful actor, a deliberate change agent. In short, God leads.

Recall, for example, this well-known incident of God's initiative and leadership. When God revealed his personal name to
Moses at the burning bush, he used a phrase suggesting strong
leadership. The disarmingly bland and sometimes puzzling description "I AM WHO I AM" (Exodus 3:14) may actually be a
causative form of the verb "to be." Translating the causative flavor
depicts a forceful, pioneering leader: "I AM THE ONE WHO
CAUSES THINGS TO HAPPEN."[3] God is a leader who makes
things happen. He acts, takes risks, blazes trails, exercises initiative, sets the pace, and serves as a catalyst for redemptive change.
All of these actions are taken thoughtfully and deliberately.

Typical of God's initiatives toward redemption, at the burning
bush he announced his plan for delivering the Hebrew people to
Moses. Read again carefully the record of the Leader's intended
actions:

> . . . I have seen the affliction . . . and heard their cry . . . I know
> their sufferings, and I have come down to deliver them. . . and
> to bring them up (to) a land flowing with milk and honey . . .
> (Exodus 3:7-8, *NIV*).

Then, God invited the stunned Moses to join him and team up in "bringing up" the Hebrew people. We know this unfolding redemptive process as the Exodus, that series of actions destined to become the Mount Everest of the Old Testament.

Leaders and followers always interact. God and other Moses-figures throughout history, leaders and followers of yesterday and today, have teamed up actively. At most, believers in the God of redemption are co-leaders and stewards of opportunities. At least, we are followers and supporters. Either role, when that role responds appropriately to the redemptive initiatives of God, is fitting for persons who in faith are willing to take the risks of making things happen.

Our faith tradition affirms God as a consistent initiative taker (Hebrews 1:1). In the Incarnation, God moved toward us and pitched his tent in our midst (John 1:11). God's Son acted assertively to empty himself and serve us through death and life; we have responded with the confession that "Jesus is Lord" (Phil. 2:5-11). The Christian faith stars God as the leading actor in redemption's drama. He makes things happen. God is *the* leader.

Describing Leadership Action

What basic actions do leaders take? What defines leadership's initiatives? Leadership is an action-oriented, interpersonal, influencing process.[4] Notice the three aspects of leadership explicitly contained in our definition.

Leaders are action-oriented. We are acting or attempting to act *for a purpose.* Mission—explicit or implicit—is basic to leadership. Leaders are visionary dreamers; we see possibilities on the horizon and reflectively choose a sense of direction. Like the old auto ad, leaders have better ideas. By definition, leaders take action and *clarify mission* for our followers.

Leaders act interpersonally. The interpersonal or relational dimension of leadership reminds us that there are no leaders without followers. Leadership is reciprocal, interactive, and exchange-based. Leaders and followers are always linked in relationship of some sort.

One political leader described leadership cynically as "finding a parade and getting in front of it." I don't like his attitude, but he's right at one point: leaders do have followers. Self-proclaimed leaders who glance over their shoulders and see no one following are leaders only in their own minds. Real leaders pay attention to the needs, interests, values, and feelings of their followers. Leaders in the Bible served their followers. By definition, leaders take action and *heighten morale*.

Leaders' actions influence others. Leaders make a difference; we are change agents. In the church, we teach, preach, counsel, evangelize, consult, plan, confront, urge, inspire, cajole, pray, listen, and encourage. Religious change agents act at the command of, react to movements of, and wait reflectively on the Spirit of God. By definition, the end product of the actions of clarifying mission and heightening morale is the *process of influence and change*.

Action: Who, Where, When?

The Bible overflows with leadership episodes or vignettes for our instruction. These twenty pivotal incidents selected for this book clearly show leaders who make things happen. Generally speaking, these leadership episodes illustrate three action roles or initiative-taking patterns.

Leaders are those persons and/or groups who take action and make things happen. We think things through, assume responsibility, show initiative, and take risks. We step to the front, set new directions, and show the way. Leaders are future-oriented and are constantly taking action to create the next generation of leaders. In short, religious leaders act redemptively to bring in the kingdom of God. Hopefully, when these leaders act in behalf of congregations, we take initiative well, with redemptive and ethical purposes in mind, at appropriate times, for the sake of the future, and in constructive ways. Leaders cause things to happen.

Followers are those persons and/or groups who respond to leaders' actions. Our responses vary widely, of course. We may participate as team leaders, submit to orders, cheer on the pacesetters, or emerge as leaders ourselves. But they act too. As in physics, leaders' actions and relationships seem to contain built-in reactions on the part of followers. Followers help things happen.

Leadership situations are settings and systems in which or circumstances for which action is required. Effective leadership action is applied to a context. Leadership involves the "wheres and whens" of places and times as well as the "whos," the personalities of leaders and followers.

Looking for Leadership Principles

Leadership episodes in the Bible reveal insights and principles that can be applied by contemporary leaders of the modern church. The approach taken to the Bible's leadership incidents in this book is more casebook than codebook, more descriptive than technical, more congregational than critical, and more applied than abstract. The texts and incidents are taken as they are recorded and interpreted as narratives with special attention to the leadership implications of each story.

Structure of the Materials

The structure of the chapter materials that follow is akin to a newspaper. Each episode is first described factually in *front-page* news fashion; the leadership applications are then noted from an *editorial* or commentary angle; and, finally, the principles are identified and summed up in concise *want-ad* style. The varied typefaces help you see when the content shifts from one theme and format to another.

This unique format offers you three ways to read this book. (1) You can take a traditional approach and read the chapters of this book from "kiver to kiver" (as we said in the Ozark Mountains). The advantage of this approach is its continuity and comprehensiveness; you take advantage of the context of the four sections of the book and can relate chapters to each other more easily. (2) You can take an "as needed" angle and read any chapter in any order—as your curiosity is awakened. The advantage of this approach is that you make the most of your motivational peaks. (3) As an unusual alternative, you might adopt an "archeological" approach and read "sideways" through the book's three strata—all the narratives first, all the commentaries next, and all the summaries of principles last.

Because the ideas in this book are intended as much for laypersons as for clergy, a variety of business and theological materials have been cited. My hope is that the more business-oriented items will inform the theologically literate reader, and the more theologically-based information will undergird the business perspective.

Read and Discuss

This book is intended both to be read reflectively and discussed thoroughly. Therefore, the leadership approaches of this book are overviewed in the discussion guides in the back of this book for teaching purposes.

Foundations:
What Makes Leaders Great?

A few years ago an airliner crashed into the Potomac River short of Washington National during a night of bad weather. As crashes go, this one was gentle. The plane neither broke up nor burned. Flight attendants immediately began evacuating the craft. A woman passenger found herself poised on a wing's edge ready to jump into the inky darkness. Suddenly, she realized she couldn't swim. When she plunged into the night, she was surprised to land on a sandbar. She reported later with great relief, "It was great to feel something solid beneath my feet!" Leaders know that feeling. We launch out into the unknown of some new adventure and are bolstered by having a stable place to stand.

Stability is crucial to leadership effectiveness. Foundations stabilize buildings and bridges. Roots undergird plants. The jet stream's steering currents guide weather fronts. Plans and processes give organizations a track to run on.

Greatness in leadership grows out of several foundational elements:

-Leaders act out of a redemptive vision.
-Leaders act from a solid self-definition.
-Leaders act with personal integrity.
-Leaders act on the basis of hard-won experience.
-Leaders act with sensitivity towards followers.
-Leaders act in highly focused ways.
-Leaders act with good timing.

These items provide a root system for effective leadership.

Look for several themes to run through the seven incidents in this section.

(1) Leaders realize Lordship precedes overlordship. Leaders, in service-oriented settings, give their allegiances to their Lord rather than demanding to be overlords. This action identifies the Lord of the kingdom, the revealer of selfhood, the anchor of values, the God of experience, the Shepherd of shepherds, the target goal, and the prompter of leadership action.

(2) Leaders are anchored in relationships and values. Look for the following threads in this section. A sense of purpose is rooted in God. Continuity is provided by leaders' experiences. Community grows out of the group being led. Concern for others guides leaders' actions. Focus based on a sense of calling. Timing triggered by the needs of followers and the demands of situations.

(3) Leaders know themselves. Note the recurrence of these ideas in the section to follow. We are self-defined, aware of our goals, sensitive to our backgrounds, know to whom we belong, understand our core goals, and read internal and external cues.

(4) Leaders function in community contexts. This section echoes with biblical references to kingdoms, nations, herds, finish lines, knocks of opportunity, and, most of all, God's kingdom and purposes. Leadership never happens in a vacuum. The interactions of leadership overflow with "whos" and "wheres"—all based on "whys."

CHAPTER I

Steering by the Rudder of a Better Idea

(Vision/Jesus and the kingdom of God in Luke 4)

Vision provides a steadying, stabilizing core for leadership. For Jesus, the kingdom of God was his guiding vision. That kingdom dream kept him consistently on course.

Vision—The Guiding Force

Imagine you're listening to relaxing music on your radio. Without warning, an announcer breaks in with "Bulletin! Bulletin!" Instantly, you feel a jolt of electric-like energy surge through your body and psyche. Then, the announcer reports, "The time has come . . . The kingdom of God is near. Repent and believe the Good News!" (Mark 1:15, *NIV*). Jesus bet his life on the vision in this dramatic headline.

The first three Gospels see the ministry of Jesus with the same eyes; for that reason we call these books the "Synoptic" or "same eyes" Gospels. We could also claim that these books are "Synotic" or "same ears" Gospels because they hear Jesus' message with the same ears. Why? Because Mark, Matthew, and Luke all begin with and focus on the same theme in Jesus' proclamation—the kingdom of God. God's kingdom was Jesus' vision, his rudder, his steering current for leadership.

Leaders need an internal guidance system, a rudder to keep them on course, a compass to point the way. For Jesus, his vision of the kingdom of God guided his leadership from the inauguration of his ministry until its end. After all, he had apparently spent the first three decades of his life clarifying how he would conduct his work once he had declared himself. When the time for the messianic ministry arrived, the direction was already set. The rudder had been locked firmly onto God's kingdom.

Luke 4 instructs us on leadership foundations. Look at the flow of the chapter. First, Jesus, full of the Holy Spirit, is confronted by the tempter and reveals four operating principles for his life and work (Luke 4:1-21). Next, he faces rejection, casts out a demon, and heals the sick (Luke 4:22-41). Then, response to his first day of ministry is so positive that the local citizenry tries unsuccessfully to persuade him to locate the home office for his work in their area. Finally, see and hear the operational vision for Jesus: "I must preach the good news of the kingdom of God . . . that is why I was sent" (Luke 4:43, *NIV*). This chapter reveals the overall structure of Jesus' ministry, principled and guided by his vision of the kingdom of God.

Take a closer look at the principles of Luke 4. Note first how each of the temptations spotlighted a principle of Jesus' work. Initially, the tempter assures him that he deserves to break his fast in style and that he should treat himself to a good meal. But Jesus refuses to adopt the "pleasure principle" because life doesn't consist of bread alone (Luke 4:4). Then, the tempter offers political clout. But Jesus turns away from the "power principle" and dedicates his worship and service exclusively to God (Luke 4:8). Finally, the tempter suggests that Jesus do a swan dive from the pinnacle of the temple and amaze the throngs when angels catch him at ground level. But Jesus rejects the "parade principle" and refuses to tempt God.

The bedrock principle of Jesus is shown, however, in the very next paragraph when he delivers his Nazareth Manifesto. Savor the action statement that zeroes in on service.

The Spirit of the Lord is on me, because he has anointed me to preach good news to the poor. He has sent me to proclaim freedom for the prisoners and recovery of sight for the blind, to release the oppressed, to proclaim the year of the Lord's favor (Luke 4:18-19, *NIV*).

Jesus chose the "service principle" for his work. Service was the approach of his work. But, as important as servanthood is to Jesus' ministry, it isn't the guiding vision or rudder. Servanthood is the "how" of Jesus' work; the kingdom of God is the "why." Principles are clues pointing to the foundational dream. In Luke 4, Jesus' leadership baseline marches straight toward the idea of the kingdom of God.

Jesus' vision statement disclosing the "why" doesn't appear until the end of Luke 4. A series of intervening events could have clouded his mind or diverted his attention along the way. Consider this rapid-fire sequence of events. His own townsmen threaten his life, an evil spirit recognizes him as "the Holy One of God" (Luke 4:34, *NIV*), the general public is awed by his power, he heals many sick persons, the demons declare him "the Son of God" (Luke 4:41, *NIV*), and the natives attempt to recruit him as their local leader. But nothing distracts Jesus. His foundation declaration spotlights the kingdom of God once again (Luke 4: 43). Don't miss how pivotal the kingdom of God was as the target of Jesus' ministry.

Jesus' nearly three-score parables are commonly considered the purest record of his teaching we have. Typically, the parables begin with the words, "The kingdom of God is like . . . " Numerous themes occur in Jesus' teaching about the kingdom, but two themes are certain. (1) The kingdom demands the sovereignty or Boss-ship of God. He's in charge and calls the shots. Leaders act. (2) The king changes life. The vision of the kingdom transforms life and makes it different. That's leadership.

Jesus put a surprise spin on leadership. He saw that all leadership is under Lordship. We choose a rudder, a foundational vision for our lives. There's something or Someone at the center or helm of our lives. We influence or lead others out of that center; we show who's the boss every time we try to lead. Luke 4 shows us that Jesus was servant of the King; we see Jesus' principles growing out of his vision. Leadership under Lordship and leadership in the service of Lordship summarizes Jesus' approach to influencing and transforming others.

What Makes for Real Leadership?

Leaders—by their vision, principles, and sense of Lordship— transform life. James McGregor Burns in Leadership *distinguishes between two types of leaders, transactors and transformers.[1] But, in fact, only transformers are real leaders.*

The first option doesn't have the vision or foundation to produce transformed followers. "Transacting leaders," like many managers, simply allot resources according to exchanges. They practice the art of compromise or quid pro quo, trading "something for something." Transactors are traders and bargainers. But the bargain is an end in itself. Beyond the bargain, there's no enduring purpose or vision holding the leader and follower together.

On the other hand, "transforming leaders" elevate, envision, mobilize, inspire, exalt, uplift, and exhort. The power of a common vision and the intensity of the engagement binds leaders and followers together for the future. Transformational leadership has a moral dimension because it ultimately "raises the level of human conduct and ethical aspiration of both leader and led, and thus it has a transforming effect on both."[2]

Leaders transform tomorrows. Napoleon described leaders as dealers in hope because they envision the future. A Methodist bishop claimed that he sold horizons. His perspective on leadership was correct. The motto of Epcot Center, "If you can dream it, you can do it," underscores leaders' future orientation. Leaders are dream merchants—first, last, and always. Leaders help others envision a preferred future and then work with others to turn the future into their shared vision.

The first task of the leader, therefore, is to focus the group's vision. Leaders help followers become more conscious of their own needs, values, self-definition, and purposes. Leaders serve their followers instead of the other way around. This act of consciousness raising calls for an unusual level of self-differentiation on the part of leaders. Leaders must be as sure of ultimate bossship as Jesus was in Luke 4. Leaders' vision, loyalties, and values provide the rudder that keeps their emotional and spiritual ships steady and on course. Incidentally, raised consciousness also requires enough independence on the part of followers so that they can freely accept ownership of their own interests. Then they can become stewards of their own self-development.

When then-President Jimmy Carter read Burns' Leadership, he realized that he'd run for and won the presidency as a transformer. Remember his call for and his vision of "an America as good as its people?" He campaigned in order to change directions, but he bogged down in detail and bureaucracy and governed as a transactor. He had intended to serve the people but had drifted into minding the government. Carter asked his cabinet members to read Burns' book and then replaced all who couldn't or wouldn't function as transformers. Transactors don't change their worlds, but transformers do.

This incident raises an intriguing, but threatening, question. What if your job security was based on one simple criterion: Do you serve as a transformer? Transformers have deliberately chosen their vision and operating principles. That's a basic message for leaders from Luke 4.

Needed: Visionary and Principled Leaders

Wanted: Leaders who have thought through their approach to and stewardship of leadership—before they are elevated to prominence.

Wanted: Leaders who realize leadership is rooted in lordship.

Wanted: Leaders who can't be tempted or diverted away from their bedrock principles because they see a clear vision.

Wanted: Leaders who have been transformed—and are, therefore, transformers instead of just transactors.

Wanted: Leaders who are willing to be evaluated according to their ability to transform followers, situations, and futures.

Wanted: Leaders who know the Boss rather than who want to boss.

Wanted: Leaders who are dream merchants and hope dealers.

* * * * *

CHAPTER II

Knowing Who You Are When Everything Is Coming Unglued

(Self-definition/Mordecai in Esther 1-10)

Self-definition keeps a leader on course when all else has jumped the track. Mordecai the Jew knew who he was and saved a nation. He's a prime example of one fact: identity makes the difference.

Knowing Who You Are

A clear personal identity is a precious possession, especially when everything comes unglued. Mordecai left a self-defined legacy because he clearly knew who he was. Savor the concluding statement from the book of Esther. Each phrase is virtually an identifier for the man described eight times in Esther simply as "the Jew."

> Mordecai the Jew
> was second in rank to King Xerxes,
> preeminent among the Jews
> and held in high esteem by his many fellow Jews,
> because he worked for the good of his people
> and spoke up for the welfare of all the Jews
> (Esther 10:3, *NIV*).

Mordecai's life turned out well, although its fabric was woven of the warp of threat and the woof of crisis. Identity explains why Mordecai survived and thrived. When you know who you are, what you do follows automatically.

Mordecai moved quietly behind the scenes during a turbulent time in Old Testament history, but made a public, long-term contribution to the survival of God's people. Think of what he did. Mordecai reared Esther, his uncle's daughter (Esther 2:7 and 15). He uncovered the assassination plot against the king and saved the ruler's life (Esther 2:21-22). He coached Esther during the Haman crisis when the Jews faced extermination (Esther 3-9). All of these feats were undertaken simply as "the Jew." All of these actions were taken without a hint of personal ambition or any demand for the limelight. In actuality, Mordecai was the real hero of the only biblical book dedicated to telling the story of the survival of the Jews. Typical of Mordecai, he moved in near anonymity and functioned as a servant in this crucial saga.

What kept Mordecai on course when he and his people faced annihilation? Did he rely on his sense of belonging to God's people? Yes, simply as the Jew. Tradition and roots? Always the Jew. The Commandments, especially the First Commandment? Yes, the Jew. Each factor undoubtedly helped shape who he was. His leadership grew directly out of his identity. Remember that Mordecai didn't lead because he sought to become a leader. He merely provided leadership out of who he was. His self-definition sustained and guided him.

There's a principle to be learned from Mordecai's leadership experience. Identity provides leaders a place to stand and a strategy from which to operate.

Leadership Rooted in Self-Definition

Ed Friedman in Generation to Generation *describes three strategies of leadership and shows why they do or don't work in social systems.¹ These three leadership approaches, systemic in nature like Paul's "body of Christ" image, are based on charismatic personalities, group consensus, and corporate health. Only one of these strategies is based on self-definition, however.*

Charismatic leadership depends on the force, attractiveness, and magnetism of the leader's personality. To its credit, charisma can energize groups, move them toward goals, and get quick responses. This strategy works best when the group is dependent, depressed, and looking for a directive rescuer. Charismatic leaders frequently personalize issues and may, therefore, polarize groups and define themselves in opposition to other persons or groups. Additionally, this leadership strategy can create a cult-like loyalty that leaves a leadership vacuum in future generations, tends to burn the leader out as he takes on too much responsibility, and attempts to clone itself in followers.

Picture a human body with its head floating detached a few inches above the neck. That depicts the charismatic leadership strategy graphically. The leader stands apart, is disconnected, and comes unstuck from the group. This lack of direct connection to followers opens the door for demagoguery when charisma goes awry.

In contrast, consensus leadership depends on the will of the group for its direction. Leaders are subsumed into the group itself. In consensus groups, fellowship tends to be rich, relationships are valued, and peaceableness usually reigns. Unfortunately, ideas and decisions tend to be reduced to the least common denominator when prophetic voices are muffled. Furthermore, a wandering herd is easily stampeded, falls prey to the emotional blackmailers who demand their way in return for not creating dissension, and fears outsiders. Comfortable and cautious groups are susceptible to the advantages and disadvantages of passive consensus leadership.

Think again of a human body. Consensus places the head inside the torso of the body. That's as grotesque as a severed head, isn't it? The leader has no vision or perspective when totally buried within the group. When the leader and the group are stuck together, the phenomenon called groupthink that tendency of fused groups to conform to their own values and behaviors, takes over and independence is sacrificed on the altar of dependence.

Finally, organic leadership links leaders and the body they try to lead. The leader and group are part of one another. Return to our image of the human body once more. Organic leadership is represented by a correct head-body relationship and connection. The head is able to define itself in relation to the larger body. Self-definition refers to "the capacity to be an 'I' while remaining connected."[2] Self-differentiation is the key to effective organic leadership.

Self-definition is apparent in quality leaders. In the Old Testament, Joshua called Israel to Shechem to renew their covenant with God. He reviewed Israel's history and then defined his own position:

> *Now fear the Lord and serve him with all faithfulness. Throw away the gods your forefathers worshiped beyond the River and in Egypt, and serve the Lord.*
> *But if serving the Lord seems undesirable to you, then choose for yourselves this day whom you will serve, whether the gods your forefathers served beyond the River, or the gods of the Amorites, in whose land you are living.*
> *But as for me and my household, we will serve the Lord. (Joshua 24:14-15, NIV).*

In the Gospels, Jesus consistently used "I" messages to define himself. For example, in a series of "I am" statements, he declared himself the bread of life (John 6:35), the light of the world (John 8: 2), the good shepherd (John 10: 11), and the resurrection and the life (John 11:25).

Powerful examples of self-defining leadership are seen beyond the Bible too. For instance, Martin Luther triggered the Reformation with his "Here I stand" position of self-differentiation. Dur-

ing the American Revolution, Patrick Henry posed his personal options: "Give me liberty, or give me death!" More recently, Martin Luther King, Jr. stirred us with his "I Have a Dream" speech. Each of these incidences illustrates how a clear personal position galvanized followers into action.

Self-definition in leadership calls for three consistent actions. (1) Leaders must remain connected to and in touch with their groups. This action is easiest for leaders to achieve. Some current leadership theorists encourage management by walking around. Visibility and accessibility are ways leaders remain in touch with and connected to their followers. The danger in connectedness for leaders, however, is becoming swallowed up by followers and following them. (2) Leaders must take well-thought out and clearly defined positions. Well-defined positions are more difficult to maintain and may tempt leaders into pressuring followers to become clones. (3) Leaders must not "twitch" by reacting anxiously to followers who want the leader to be less self-differentiated. Twitching is so natural that leaders are prone to overreact, abandon their self-defining positions, and lose themselves in the group.

Contrast the organic strategy with charisma and consensus. Charisma stresses "I-ness" without "we-ness" and majors in "you" statements. Consensus emphasizes "we-ness" without "I-ness" and uses "us" statements primarily. Both the charisma and the consensus ends of the leadership spectrum are flawed systemically. Organic leadership features "I-ness" with "we-ness" and applies "I" statements to the life of the body. This third strategy of leadership based on self-definition is healthier for leaders and followers, and, consequently, for the overall social system.

The Value of Self-Definition

Wanted: Leaders who have discovered who they are and operate consistently out of their self-definitions.

Wanted: Leaders whose comfort with and confidence in their identities allow them to function either behind the scenes or in the foreground with equal ease and constancy.

Wanted: Leaders who resist "I-centered" dictatorial and "we-centered" group-absorbed approaches to leadership because these strategies are neither who they are nor healthy for their groups.

Wanted: Leaders who will commit themselves to self-definition while remaining in touch with their followers, maintaining clear positions on issues, and keeping their anxiety in check.

* * * * *

CHAPTER III

Living with Integrity When You're Tempted to Cut Corners

(Integrity/Joseph in Genesis 39)

Joseph developed an internal consistency that guided him when he was tempted toward unethical behavior. His core values were, however, the product of a long and painful maturation process.

Come to Bed with Me!

At times Joseph's life was the pits—literally. What's worse, he brought most of his woes on himself. As my Grandma described people like Joseph, he was "too big for his britches. Someone should take that kid down a notch or two!" Joseph was an arrogant teenager. He was heading for a fall.

The young Joseph wasn't conscious of what was happening in others' lives. Rather, he acted like an accident looking for a place to happen. Joseph was a tattletale (Genesis 37:2), his father's obvious favorite (Genesis 37:3), and a tactless braggart when he told about his dreams of dominance over his brothers (Genesis 37:5-11). That's a recipe for instant trouble.

Trouble is exactly what exploded Joseph's blind ambition when his brothers hatched a plot that got Joseph's full attention. That plot, for the first time, put Joseph in an actual pit, a dry cistern. The cistern itself was an alternative to outright murder. But, in his brothers' estimation, Joseph was a dead man anyway. The odds of living very long as a slave in Egypt were extremely long. Bloodying Joseph's long-sleeved, princely coat, the brothers deceived Father Jacob into thinking his favorite son had been killed by animals. Their news left the old man in long-term mourning (Genesis 37:12-35).

Meanwhile, Joseph was growing up fast in a slow-moving Midianite caravan headed for Egypt. Slaves aren't the center of attention. When someone else owns your life, you are no one's favorite, enjoy no fancy coats, and dare not dream of domination. Joseph was "getting taken down a notch or two." On this journey, the arrogance in Joseph was humbled and the youth became a man.

Joseph had one thing going for him, however. He had cultivated his inner life. Even as a youngster, he dreamed and remembered his dreams. These dreams gave meaning to his life and sensitized him to the stirrings of God within him. These insights defined and directed his destiny. When Joseph was sold into the service of Potiphar, the captain of Pharaoh's guard, a certain aura became obvious about the young Hebrew.

> The Lord was with Joseph and he prospered, and he lived in the house of his Egyptian master. When his master saw that the Lord was with him and the Lord gave him success in everything he did, Joseph found favor in his eyes and became his attendant. Potiphar put him in charge of his household, and he entrusted to his care everything he owned. From the time he put him in charge of all his household and of all that he owned, the Lord blessed the household of the Egyptian because of Joseph. The blessing of the Lord was on everything Potiphar had, both in the house and in the field (Genesis 39:2-5, *NIV*).

External blessings were rooted in internal integrity. The young man who earlier didn't notice—or care to notice—what was happening outside his own life now banked on the inner support of God. He was soon to need all the inner resources he could muster.

Potiphar's wife noticed how handsome and well-built Joseph was. She asked him to have sex with her. Surprised by her proposition, Joseph refused on two grounds: she was another man's wife, and he would not sin against God (Genesis 39:6-9). Joseph's inner gyroscope guided him away from his master's wife, although Joseph had free rein with every other aspect of Potiphar's household. Like Adam and Eve in the Garden of Eden, everything was available to be enjoyed—except for what was dedicated to another.

Potiphar's wife pursued Joseph, but he kept turning her down and began to avoid her. Then, one day she caught him alone with her in the otherwise empty house, caught him by his underwear, and insisted again, "Come to bed with me!" (Genesis 39:11-12). Joseph ran out of the room naked. He might have been embarrassed, but he had preserved his integrity intact. Unfortunately, Potiphar's wife still had his underwear and used it to frame Joseph (Genesis 39:13-20). In short order, he found himself in another pit, a prison where he stayed for thirteen years.

Even in the pits again, "the Lord was with Joseph and gave him success in whatever he did" (Genesis 39:23, *NIV*). In fact, the self-absorbed young man matured into a self-aware adult who realized God's hand in his life. Sensitivity to his interior life undoubtedly helped Joseph interpret others' dreams and escape the pit of prison. Later, when he would rise to power and reveal his real identity to his terrified brothers, he interpreted his life in Egypt as God's plan (Genesis 45:4-8). His inner resources gave him the integrity not to cut corners when he was tempted.

Integrity: Foothold for Problem Solving

Leaders spend most of their time and energy solving problems. That's the claim of Leadership and the Quest for Integrity.[1] *In order to make sound decisions, leaders constantly rely on their central, consistent core of values, their basis for integrity. It's integrity that enables leaders to operate from strong personal beliefs and behave predictably day in and day out.*

*Max DePree defines integrity as "a fine sense of one's obliga-
tions."* [2] *Integrity grows out of constancy in personal values and
wholesome organizational aims. Integrity is made plain in leaders' actions, the working link between personal beliefs and organizational goals. An American prisoner of war in Korea, General
Dean, wrote his son to maintain his integrity above all. Why?
Because to lose one's integrity, in his opinion, was to lose everything.*

*Personal values are demonstrated in ethical, fair, and honest
behavior as well as positive belief in others. But, most important,
values are seen clearly in the vision a leader possesses—or, more
likely—the vision that possesses the leader. Vision provides a
directing compass and determines which risks are to be taken.
Joseph's values and vision sustained him when his life was going
well and when it was in the pits.*

*Organizational aims are built on high ethical standards show-
ing respect, trust, and compassion. These goals show integrity
when they demonstrate (1) open communication, (2) family spirit,
(3) a free environment, and (4) meritocracy. Open communication
provides settings where strong opinions can be debated with
emotion but without rancor. Family spirit is reflected in a deeply
shared sense of purpose. A free environment balances authority
and responsibility. Meritocracy helps talented people excel, become empowered, and gain rewards based on ability. Joseph rose
to prominence on the basis of what he could do for the Egyptian
nation; he was fortunate that Pharaoh appreciated professional
abilities and rewarded them. But what Joseph did for the nation
was based on who he was as a person. Leaders are rarely better
leaders than they are persons.*

Finding and Counting on Core Values

Wanted: Leaders who relate tactfully and fairly—even when they have special gifts.

Wanted: Leaders who will cultivate their emotional gardens and identify the stirrings of God.

Wanted: Leaders who don't have to be stars—but can take center stage when the spotlight falls on them.

Wanted: Leaders who respect people and property—and know which is which.

Wanted: Leaders who are stable enough to survive the pits and pinnacles of life with steadiness.

Wanted: Leaders whose values and vision give them—and their organizations—integrity.

* * * * *

CHAPTER IV

Graduating from the School of Hard Knocks

(Experience/Jacob in Genesis 25-35)

Do we really learn from experience? Learning by trial and error is a common way to gain leadership experience. But it's one of the tougher ways to absorb life's lessons. As Jacob discovered from hard experience during his life, the colors of the School of Hard Knocks are black and blue and "fight, fight, fight" is more than just its pep song.

Short Cuts and Long Detours

Experience opens our eyes. Experience moves us from ignorance of our ignorance to awareness of our awareness. Trial-and-error experience, although slow and even painful at points, can be very educational. In fact, trial-and-error experience—when enriched by actual learning—can be transformed into trial and success. It isn't practice that makes perfect. Rather, as the late football coach Vince Lombardi claimed, perfect practice makes perfect.

Jacob's leadership experience demonstrates an array of trials and can virtually be depicted as a ledger sheet of errors on the one hand and of successes on the other. Jacob proves the old saying, "God can hit straight licks with crooked sticks." Note his errors first and then his successes.

"If it weren't for bad luck, I'd have no luck at all!" That old lament could have been Jacob's personal motto. Jacob's trials and errors were frequently more a result of his deliberate choices than simple bad luck. At times, Jacob was the J.R. Ewing of the Old Testament. Look at this listing of experience gained through Jacob's "errors."

- Even while in the womb, Jacob was crushed or "jostled" (Genesis 25:22, *NIV*) by his unborn brother.
- At birth, Jacob lost out to his twin and was born second when Esau, whose name can mean "to press or squeeze," literally squeezed himself into the world first.
- The short form of Jacob's name can be translated "heel" or "supplanter" and suggested his character trait of tripping up people—and himself.
- Jacob cunningly traded food for Esau's privileges as first born, gaining a double portion of the family's estate and leadership of the clan (Genesis 25:27-34).
- Jacob, implementing his mother's scheme, stole Esau's blessing by deceiving father Isaac (Genesis 27:1-40).
- Facing Esau's understandable rage, Jacob fled from home for security purposes (Genesis 27:42-46).
- Jacob met his match in the wily Laban and found himself married to Leah, "the cow," instead of Rachel, "the little lamb" (Genesis 29:20-30).
- After Jacob was married to Rachel, she was thought to be barren and unable to produce heirs (Genesis 29:31).
- Jacob's four marriages created dissension in his household (Genesis 30).
- Laban agreed that all of the marked livestock would belong to Jacob and then craftily removed all the spotted breeding stock from his flocks (Genesis 30:25-43).
- Returning home after twenty years on the run, the fearful Jacob is confronted by Esau and 400 men but, to his relief, discovers he has been forgiven (Genesis 31:22-42).

—The rape of Jacob's daughter and the subsequent trickery and treacherous revenge of his sons against the offending Shechemites uncovers Jacob's core concern—his safety (Genesis 34).

—Jacob apparently loses his favorite son, Joseph, and jeopardizes the covenant again (Genesis 37).

From a leadership viewpoint, this litany of deviousness and disaster sometimes makes us wonder how Jacob and his kind could have become the heroes of the faith in the Bible (Hebrews 11). (1) Remember the blunt question that echoes implicitly throughout patriarchal history: Can God keep his covenant promises? Think of the challenges. Could God bless the world through persons who were flawed and disobedient? Could God raise up an ancestry as numerous as the sands of the seas when wombs were barren? Could God give land to nomadic herdsman? Yes. Yes. Yes. Genesis reminds us that nothing is too difficult for God to accomplish (Genesis 18:14). (2) People frequently mature as they learn about themselves, others, and God. The patriarchs weren't perfect, but ultimately they learned what God wanted of them and—in fits and starts—generally did what God had covenanted with them to do.

Now, consider the "successes" side of Jacob's experience ledger. The third of the Hebrew patriarchs, in spite of his mistakes, became Israel both in name and through his twelve sons.

—Jacob gained Isaac's final blessing legitimately (Genesis 28:1).

—Jacob's ladder dream assured him of God's blessing and protection (Genesis 28::2-15).

—Jacob met, married, and loved Rachel, the eventual mother of the favored Joseph (Genesis 29). Later, Jacob left his clan's leadership and the stewardship of the covenant to Joseph (Genesis 49:22-26).

— Jacob became a person of means (Genesis 30:25-43).

—Jacob was changed physically and transformed spiritually during his night-long wrestling match with God and his own conscience (Genesis 32:22-32).

—Jacob returned to Bethel, cleansed his life and that of his family, and renewed his covenant with God (Genesis 35: 1-8).

—Jacob found Joseph again, reunited his family, and was assured of God's blessing (Genesis 46:3-4).

Jacob's greatest success was becoming the new man Israel as a result of his struggle with God and the covenant nation Israel through the ancestry of his twelve sons. "The Tripper" learned from his experiences and eventually emerged as "The Wrestler Who Prevailed" (Genesis 32:28), the leader of a redemptive minority.

Experience—The Best Teacher?

Jacob is a good example of an important lesson: life isn't what happens to you but what you do with what happens to you. Experience by itself isn't necessarily the best teacher. Experience—when undergirded by learning—is, however, a great instructor in living. How, then, can experience help us define success, deal with failure, and make ethical decisions?

Experience helps each of us define success. For most of us, success is more a journey than a destination, a process more than a product. According to Maya Angelou, "In the struggle lies the joy." That is, if we aren't happy with and satisfied by the daily flow of our lives, we aren't likely to be pleased with the final outcome.

It does, however, take time for the contours of our lives to emerge and shape our values. The patriarchs are typical of other religious leaders like Moses, Jesus, Augustine, and Luther. All were mature persons with lots of miles on them before they found the life niche for which they are now remembered as successes in faith and life.

Life's experience radically changed Jacob's view of success. For the majority of his life, Jacob concentrated on gaining things —a birthright, a blessing, a beauty, a bankroll, and a bloodless reunion. By the twilight of his life, he was becoming focused on God's covenant with him and his family.

Some losers become winners by learning from their failures. *Take James W. Arnett as one example. He flunked out of Tennessee Tech with a near-zero grade point average. His father, a retired Marine, demanded that James get a job and pay back $1400 of tuition costs. Fearful that he was on his way to becoming a loser in life, Arnett was stirred to action and to discipline.*

Cooking hamburgers and stirring soup for a new restaurant chain called Shoney's provided James first with a minimum wage job and then with a career. He had found something he liked to do and could do well. James did whatever was needed; he cooked and swept up the place, learning the business from the floor up literally. James was promoted to kitchen manager and eventually store manager. After twenty years with Shoney's, James Arnett is now president and chief operating officer. Experience with his company was a fundamental reason Arnett was selected as Shoney's leader. He has transformed an early failure into an ultimate success. Many leaders rise like the phoenix from the ashes of their early failures.

Experience, even bad experiences, can inform our ability to make ethical decisions. *Kenneth Blanchard and Norman Vincent Peale in* The Power of Ethical Management[1] *offer an "ethical check." They identify three questions their experience has taught them to use when facing ethical issues. (1) "Is it legal?" reminds us that civil laws, organizational policies, professional standards, and cultural norms always apply when moral concerns arise. A "No" answer to this first question of legality usually makes the remaining two inquiries irrelevant. (2) "Is it balanced?" explores matters of fair play and equity both present and long-term. This* *issue is especially critical for interdependent groups, like families, congregations, and teams, since win-lose resolutions ultimately undercut the entire group's morale and productivity. (3) "How do I feel about myself in relation to this issue?" focuses ethical questions on our self-concept. How, for example, would I feel if my action was broadcast on the evening news so that my family and friends knew what I'd done?*

Jacob could have made good use of these questions and their applications. Rather than taking moral and spiritual shortcuts, he learned that God resolves seemingly impossible impasses without our intervention—and without our mistakes. As Jacob's favorite son Joseph later interpreted his brothers' actions and God's intention: You intended evil, but God brought good (Genesis 50: 20).

Saving the Lessons of Losses

Wanted: Leaders who recognize their humanity, but are not willing to use human foibles as an excuse for their mistakes.

Wanted: Leaders whose concept of success is built on the designs of God.

Wanted: Leaders who learn **from** their errors rather than only learning **about** those mistakes.

Wanted: Leaders who resist making life a series of ethical shortcuts.

Wanted: Leaders who build life altars at their personal Bethels and Peniels to mark their experiences with God, their renewal events, and their process of maturity.

* * * * *

CHAPTER V

Valuing Followers Too!

(Followership/Ezekiel in Ezekiel 34)

Leaders need followers. In our kind of world, the mistreated or ignored follower soon follows no more, leaving leaders with no one to lead. Effective leaders know that followers count too—and value them accordingly.

Shepherd-Oriented Leaders vs. Sheep-Oriented Leaders

Sheep. Shepherds. It's probably been at least two or three hours since your last in-depth conversation about the care and feeding of farm animals. Our modern urban world doesn't think about sheep and shepherds much, does it? But, the Old Testament world was at ease with images of hillsides and herds. Why not? Sheep were the primary source of wealth and livelihood for the pastoral peoples of biblical times.

The Bible depicts sheep-and-shepherd relationships with appreciation and high expectations. Typically, sheep were described as affectionate animals with "laid back" temperaments. Additionally, they were portrayed as poor at self-defense, requiring constant supervision. Consequently, shepherds knew their sheep and made sure they were fed and protected. Ideally, there was a kindly, friendly quality to this man-and-animal relationship. No wonder

the Psalmist said movingly: "The Lord is my shepherd, I shall not
be in want" (Psalm 23:1, *NIV*).

Ezekiel, however, was using the sheep-and-shepherd metaphor
as a direct description of leaders and followers. He saw a troublesome relationship between the leaders and followers in the Israel of
his day. Some leaders, he observed, were "shepherd-oriented" and
others were "sheep-oriented." Nowhere is this contrast drawn more
starkly than in Ezekiel 34. Don't lose one important perspective
on this picture: this withering allegory from Ezekiel is in the more
"hopeful" portion of his prophetic book.

Ezekiel blistered those "shepherd-oriented" leaders who
sought position and exercised authority for their own needs and
ends. Note the list of charges against these power wielders,
charges about how followers were used and abused.

The "shepherd-oriented" leaders were selfish:

> Woe to the shepherds of Israel who only take care of them-
> selves! Should not shepherds take care of the flock? (Ezekiel
> 34:2, *NIV*).

They were callous:

> You have not strengthened the weak or healed the sick or
> bound up the injured. You have not brought back the strays or
> searched for the lost. You have ruled them harshly and bru-
> tally (Ezekiel 34:3-4, *NIV*).

They were self-absorbed:

> The sheep "were scattered because there was no shepherd, and
> when they were scattered they became food for all the wild
> animals. My sheep wandered over all the mountains and on
> every high hill. They were scattered over the whole earth, and
> no one searched or looked for them" (Ezekiel 34:5-6, *NIV*).

They were users:

> Is it not enough for you to feed on the good pasture? Must
> you also trample the rest of your pasture with your feet? Is it
> not enough for you to drink clear water? Must you also mud-
> dy the rest with your feet? Must my flock feed on what you
> have trampled and drink what you have muddied with your
> feet? (Ezekiel 34:18-19, *NIV*).

They were merciless:

> . . . you shove with flank and shoulder, butting all the weak
> sheep with your horns until you have driven them away. . .
> (Ezekiel 34:21, *NIV*).

"Pay attention to the sheep!" was Ezekiel's straightforward
demand. Taking advantage of followers was foreign to Ezekiel's
faith. He was convinced that followers count too. Ezekiel believed in a holy God and likely would have agreed with Abraham
Heschel that callousness is the root of sin.

Ezekiel points out that shepherds are held accountable for the
welfare of the sheep, that leaders must have their followers at heart
(Ezekiel 34:10). In sharp contrast to "me first" leaders, leaders
who are "sheep-oriented" take a distinctive approach to their
followers.

They are caring and just (Ezekiel 34:7-16), can distinguish
sheep from goats (Ezekiel 34: 17), help transform the leadership
setting (Ezekiel 34:25-27), and create an atmosphere rich in security and resources (Ezekiel 34:28-29). The holy God declares
himself a "sheep-oriented" leader:

> I myself will tend my sheep and have them lie down . . . I will
> search for the lost and bring back the strays. I will bind up the
> injured and strengthen the weak, but the sleek and the strong I
> will destroy. I will shepherd the flock with justice (Ezekiel
> 34:15-16, *NIV*).

Ezekiel makes no apology in his call for follower-oriented leaders for Israel, does he? The God who is Sovereign also clearly shares that preference. God had commanded Ezekiel to "prophesy against the shepherds of Israel" (Ezekiel 34:1, *NIV*). That prophesy concludes:

> ... they will know that I, the Lord their God, am with them and that they, the house of Israel, are my people ... You are my sheep, the sheep of my pasture ... and I am your God ... (Ezekiel 34:30-31, *NIV*).

Echoes of Ezekiel 34 resound in Jesus' powerful "good shepherd" statement of leader-follower relationships in John 10:11.

> I am the good shepherd. I know my sheep and my sheep know me—just as the Father knows me and I know the Father—and I lay down my life for the sheep (John 10:14-15).

Keeping Followers in the Forefront

Tragically, little has been said about followers in current leadership studies. Most studies of leadership are focused on leaders and, secondarily, on leadership situations. Followers are the forgotten women and men in the leadership equation. Ezekiel knew the feeling. Likewise, Ezekiel would have said "amen" to John Haggai's assertion, "Ultimately, the search for the good shepherd is also the search for the good flock."[1]

Obviously, there are no leaders where there are no followers. Leaders—if they choose to be effective—keep followers constantly in the forefront of their thinking and operating. Heller and Van Til have it right: "Good leadership enhances followers, just as good followership enhances leaders."[2]

*Leadership has traditionally operated from at least three behavioral science and theological models that are now beginning to fade. The **kingly, vertical, over-under model** of authority and* *dependent, superior and subordinate, and master and servant is passing from effectiveness. A more participatory, "side-by-side approach" is emerging from today's flatter organizational structures. The **prophetic, solitary, do-it-by-myself** model is giving way to a "together approach" necessary in a complicated world, using more interdependency, team-orientation, and mutual assistance. The **warrior, competitor, adversarial** model is yielding slowly to an "on your side approach," stressing collaboration through the sharing of resources, seeking consultation, and pooling abilities.[3] Good shepherds have something to teach us in the transition to newer leadership models.*

Ralph Stayer, CEO of Johnsonville Foods, Inc., of Sheboygan, Wisconsin and managing partner of Leadership Dynamics, a consulting group specializing in change management, uses an animal metaphor to describe how he worked for higher commitment among his company's employees. Stayer noted that while his company was thriving, his employees were unmotivated.

Stayer had a vision of what he wanted for his workers. He wished for employees who would fly like geese; his ideal organizational chart visualized the "V" of geese on the wing. He wanted individuals who knew the common goal, took turns leading, and adjusted to the task at hand. Stayer wished for workers who would fly in a wedge and land in waves. Instead, he had a herd of buffalo. Deep down, he really expected his employees to follow him blindly. Frontier history, however, reminded him that buffalo hunters slaughtered herds by finding and killing the leader. When the leader was gone, the herd milled around waiting for instructions and could be killed off one at a time. So Stayer set out to turn buffalo into geese. It turned out to be a tougher change process than he anticipated.

First, Stayer abdicated decision-making control to his management team. He found out they spent their time trying to read his mind, while he really wanted them to make the decisions he would have made. Then, Stayer started defining the vision of the company and managing the corporate context. He concentrated on systems and structures. By way of systems, he turned quality control over to the production people and saw ownership of quality skyrocket. By way of structure, Stayer created work teams and watched as "I'll catch you doing something wrong" attitudes changed to "Let's improve the way we do things" atmospheres. The result? Stayer reports that his employees' "general level of commitment is now as high or higher than my own."[4]

In summary, Stayer led with his followers at heart when he . . .

(1) wanted more for *his people (rather than just more from them),*

(2) involved them more in the dreaming and planning processes,

(3) gave the decision making process over to the implementers,

(4) equalized accountability and resources,

(5) rewarded performance directly,

(6) created work teams, and

(7) made quality results everybody's business.

That's shepherding with the sheep in mind!

Stayer has put a "The Question is the Answer" plaque on his desk and tried to make his company a learning organization. "Life is aspiration. Learning, striving people are happy people and good workers."[5] That's a radical view of followership. Ezekiel would have been proud!

Growing Corporate Shepherds

Wanted: Leaders who genuinely care about the needs and aspirations of their followers.

Wanted: Leaders who know that leaders and followers relate interdependently.

Wanted: Leaders who are willing to create leader-follower atmospheres that develop and benefit both parties.

Wanted: Leaders who appreciate the fact that, in any given situation, followers are largely leaders-in-training.

***** * * * *

CHAPTER VI

Sprinting through the Tape

(Focus/Paul in Philippians 3)

Effective leaders are focused persons. They, like Paul, have a concentrated, "this one thing I do," perspective on their life targets.

Running the Race Fully

I heard a world-class sprinter tell one of the secrets of his success. He claimed some one-hundred meter runners lose their form and fade at the end of a race because mentally they prepare to run only ninety-five meters. These short-sighted runners begin to lean and lunge too soon and frequently stagger out of balance the final few steps, attempting to fall across the tape. However, the world-class sprinter reported that he set out to run one hundred and five meters in his mind and focused his concentration on continuing to stride across the finish line and right through the tape.

In Philippians 3, Paul uses a sports metaphor—a sprinter in full stride—to describe his life target of a mature knowledge of Christ. He observes that he hasn't won the blue ribbon yet. In order to reach his ultimate goal, Paul focuses on just one aim. Erasing all distracting past victories and defeats from his mind, he sprints through the tape ahead of him to claim the first place award. Visualize a runner as you read Paul's goal statement:

... one thing I do: Forgetting what is behind and straining toward what is ahead, I press on toward the goal to win the prize for which God has called me heavenward in Christ Jesus (Philippians 3:13-14, *NIV*).

Keeping focused on goals isn't easy—especially if you've had as many wins and losses as Paul. Think of his life as a ledger sheet with a long list of defeats capable of triggering doubts and distractions, on the one hand, and an even longer list of achievements creating their own addictive atmosphere, on the other hand.

2 Corinthians 11:16-33 records only one "for instance" debit sheet of Paul's defeating experiences, situations that would have crushed a lesser man and kept him from running his current race. Note these losses: given one hundred and ninety-five lashes with scourges, beaten with rods three times, shipwrecked three times, stoned once, cast adrift at sea once, and frequently endangered as a traveler. Yet Paul considered his scars as credentials and put them behind him. Losses weren't defeating distractions for Paul.

On the credit side, Paul's life ledger contains victorious entries that would have encouraged most of us average folks to retire and live out of our memories. Given Paul's record of accomplishments, it must have been a temptation to become addicted to and distracted by his achievements. Consider this partial list of his breakthrough victories: the greatest of the first-century Christian missionaries, extending the Gospel to persons of varied backgrounds; the most outstanding theologian of the early church; author of half of the New Testament; church planter *par excellence*; problem solver for persons and congregations. Paul had enjoyed more than his share of wins, but he wasn't diverted from his primary goal for all his success. Rather, he remained fixed on the tape at the end of the sprinter's lane.

Focus: One Thing I Do

Management guru Tom Peters describes another way leaders can "run through the tape." He urges leaders to develop and be ready at a moment's notice to deliver a "stump speech." [1] A stump speech is a brief statement of fundamental vision. It's specific, concrete, graphic, highly focused, and, hopefully, contagious. And, any time leaders have a forum of one person or a crowd, they seize that opportunity to jump up on a stump and give their speech. These leaders act, in the words of Napoleon, as "dealers in hope." (Note that I'm pointing toward values deep enough to stir hope rather than stimulate hype.) Leaders intend for their vision to ignite the imaginations of their followers. Then, both leader and follower become focused on a common goal. They sprint down the same track toward the same finish line.

Sprinting through the tape maintains a focus in life. Paul's "this one thing I do" perspective suggests some principles for leaders to practice.

Leaders put yesterday behind them. *Some events—positive and negative—are difficult to lay aside.*

Have you ever met persons who have had outstanding early successes in life—and couldn't or wouldn't stop allowing those victories to dominate their daily lives in the present? I knew a former college homecoming queen who, when her youth began to wane, spent up to four hours each day on make-up and her beauty routine. Her life continued to be defined by one bright autumn football Saturday a quarter century earlier. She was becoming a bitter, middle-aged woman who lived in a community where no one remembered the Big Game when she had worn the crown. She could not and would not forget what was behind.

Leaders know life is a mix of good and bad, of highs and lows, and chalk up yesterday to experience. They recognize that old trees became old by their ability to bend with the wind. Otherwise, old trees break down. Like martial arts experts who use others' momentum to lend the impetus for their throws, leaders go with the flow and refuse to be distracted by yesterday's booms or busts.

Leaders choose a goal for today. *They operate by plans and priorities. They refuse to be tyrannized by either the trivial or the urgent issue.*

Goals determine life's direction. I'm amused by the old story of two farmer neighbors. When one visited the other, he noticed six targets drawn on the barn door. Each target had a bullet hole exactly in the center. "Wow," remarked the visitor, "I didn't realize what a good shot you are!" "Oh," replied the host, "I don't shoot so well. I shoot first and draw the bull's eye later!"

Unfortunately, some leaders become too random in their lives. Whatever the day brings spontaneously forms their "to do" list. As a friend of mine reported, "At one time in my life, my goal was to handle whatever the postman delivered." Selecting a priority and planning around that priority will offer leaders a more pro-ductive focus.

Leaders aim for tomorrow. *Leaders take the long look. They think strategically and developmentally. Leaders build for the future.*

A bishop was travelling by train and fell into conversation with a group of salespersons. The bishop was bright, expressive, and compelling. He was also dressed in a business suit without any of the identifiers of his vocation. The sales people mistook the bishop for another sales representative. One asked the bishop, "What's your line? What do you sell?" The bishop answered instantly, "I sell horizons!" That's a leader's response—because the future is the currency of leadership.

Going for the Gold

Wanted: Leaders who have identified the "one thing" in their lives—and keep on pursuing it with excellence.

Wanted: Leaders who are one hundred and five meter sprinters and remain willing to attempt a bit more in life.

Wanted: Leaders who can appreciate wins and losses and who, after learning from their victories and defeats, put both behind them and move ahead toward their goals.

Wanted: Leaders who have a stump speech to sharpen vision and move followers to action.

* * * * *

CHAPTER VII

Timing —
The Right Action
at the Right Moment

(Timing/Jesus in the Gospels)

Time and timing aren't the same. Effective leaders know the difference. Leaders understand their time. In fact, Winston Churchill claimed, "Leadership is first and foremost a matter of being in touch with one's times." True. But, more important, leaders have a sense of timing. In fact, timing is the key ingredient that made Jesus an unerring leader.

Time . . . and Timing

The Bible depicts time and timing. Time is *chronos*, or the stuff of clocks and calendars. *Chronos* deals with duration, the passage of time. Timing, on the other hand, is a strikingly different matter. *Kairos* the Bible calls it. *Kairos* deals with ripeness, knocks of opportunity, and moments brimming over with potential, expectancy, and readiness. When Jesus announced his ministry, he declared his *kairos* and demonstrated his sense of timing: "The time has come . . . The kingdom is near. Repent and believe the good news!" (Mark 1:15, *NIV*).

Timing is the secret of Jesus' effectiveness as a leader. He knew his times; he understood calendars and cultures. His genius as a leader, however, involved timing. Jesus sensed his role, the needs of his followers, and the demands of the various situations in which he ministered so accurately that he applied the most effective approach consistently. To use one leader style model,[1] Jesus was a Catalyst when that style was appropriate, a Commander when that was the needed style, an Encourager when that approach was timely, and a Hermit on the few occasions when that style was applicable. He used each style option with impeccable timing. Consider these examples.

Jesus was a Catalyst most of the time. He had a keen sense of mission, and his concern for others caused him to maintain a focus on morale too. The kingdom of God, the central theme in Jesus' teaching and ministry, formed the core mission and obsession of his life and work. He called his audiences to become citizens of God's kingdom. He sent out the seventy to join with him as catalysts for the peace of the kingdom:

> When you enter a town and are welcomed, eat what is set before you. Heal the sick who are there and tell them 'The kingdom of God is near you' (Luke 10:8-9, *NIV*).

When Jesus declared his time hadn't arrived and then turned the water into wine, he demonstrated his catalytic approach. His greatest catalytic acts were the Cross and the Empty Tomb. His reconciling atonement merged mission and morale perfectly and was a consummate leadership initiative.

On some occasions, however, Jesus functioned as a Commander leader. When he cleansed the Temple, he acted in Commander fashion (John 2:16 and Mark 11:15). When he calmed the sea, he was a Commander (Mark 4:39). When he cursed the fig tree, his only destructive miracle, he acted as a Commander (Mark 12:12-26). When he directed his disciples to make other disciples in the Great Commission, he was a Commander (Matthew 28:18-20). In these situations, mission reigned and was not negotiable. Jesus called the shots. He commanded when circumstances made directive action appropriate.

But, he also led as an Encourager when emphasizing morale was the primary concern. The High Priestly Prayer in John 17 demonstrates his Encourager style. Jesus loved the little children and healed the sick. Besides, Jesus broke up every funeral procession he encountered—Jairus' daughter (Mark 5:21-43), the sole son of the widow of Nain (Luke 7:11-17), and Lazarus (John 11:1-44). When supportive action was timely, Jesus' Encourager dimension showed itself.

Occasionally, Jesus filled the Hermit role. Read Mark's Gospel through in one sitting, and you'll see a rhythm of intensity and respite in Jesus' approach to ministry. Mark's energetic, fast-moving, "motion picture" style highlights the contrast between activity and retreat. Jesus correctly used the Hermit role only for temporary refreshment before returning to the fray (Mark 6:32, 46 and John 7:10). He saw that Hermits stay focused neither on the long-term mission or group morale and that the role, beyond brief rest and recreation periods, isn't a timely leadership style.

Timing, then, determines appropriate leader actions. Timing determined when Jesus used each leadership style. A sense of *kairos* guided his relationships with his followers and his reaction to ministry opportunities.

Timing and Appropriate Flexibility

Leadership is no "one size fits all" proposition. There is no single best leader style for all situations. Consequently, Jesus used "style flex"[2] *appropriately. Style flex is the art and science of deliberately and/or intuitively adjusting one's leader approach to the unique demands of a given leadership incident. In other words, leadership is timing to a considerable extent. Therefore, leaders ordinarily take responsibility for applying style flexibly because one leader can bend more easily than a group or institution.*

Sometimes style flex is a matter of the head. It becomes a more analytical, deliberate, or logical decision. On other occa-

sions, style flex is more intuitive, a matter of "gut-feel," or the spontaneous application of our sixth sense. In these cases, we may react to a situation with an immediate, heart-felt, "this is the right action" decision. Good leaders use both their heads and hearts to take soundings of their followers and settings and to make their style flex selections.

Whether reasoned or reactive, pacesetters soon learn that leader styles must mesh well with followers and with situations—if we are to be effective. Each leader style fits some circumstances well. The Catalyst style, the broadest and most balanced approach, works best when diverse groups and mass involvement are timely. The Commander style, emphasizing mission primarily, can stabilize chaos and confront inertia. The Encourager style, stressing morale mostly, is able to bind up wounds and deal with divided groups. The Hermit style, really an abdication of leadership for survival purposes generally, creates a leadership vacuum, but it allows leaders to catch their breath emotionally and to let groups declare a moratorium on pressurized decision making. Again, Jesus' genius in leadership was in using the most effective leader style for his followers and for the ministry challenges he faced.

A few months after an advanced leadership laboratory had been completed, a friend described a major learning he'd gained from the lab. "My church was saved from a major schism by the lab. Beforehand, I rushed into every crisis determined to rescue the situation. In this case, I waited until I understood the dynamics of the conflict before I acted. In other words, I learned and used better timing." That reflects an attitude closer to Jesus' approach to leadership.

Solving Leadership Puzzles

Wanted: Leaders who appreciate the *chronos* of their times and cultures.

Wanted: Leaders who, because they are alert to *kairos*, have a sense of timing.

Wanted: Leaders who are tuned into the unique demands of followers and settings in each leadership situation.

Wanted: Leaders who know about and appreciate the range of leader styles options.

Wanted: Leaders who are committed to style flex.

Wanted: Leaders who let their heads inform their hearts and their hearts educate their heads on leader style choices and applications.

* * * * *

Styles, Stance, and Strategy:
How Do Great Leaders Operate?

If foundational values give leaders a place to stand, functional skills provide leaders with a basis for operating. Leader styles, a leadership stance, and a sense of strategy offer pacesetters ways to operate.

Marksmanship and leadership share several parallels. Some leaders seem to spend all their effort readying weapons and targets. Other leaders take great care in aiming and drawing their bead. A few leaders fire and achieve effectiveness. Any marksman knows "ready" doesn't hit the bull's eye. Neither does "ready, aim." Only "ready, aim, fire" has the potential of hitting the target. Great leaders prepare, aim carefully, and pull the trigger. That's the only way for leaders to operate.

Great leaders operate in "ready, aim, fire" fashion with consistent savvy and perspective.

—Leaders act with style balance.
—Leaders act with appropriate style directiveness.
—Leaders act with appropriate style supportiveness.
—Leaders act with appropriate style flexibility.
—Leaders act out of a servant stance.
—Leaders act strategically.

These ingredients undergird an effective operational approach to leadership.

Several operational themes recur in the six chapters of this section. Since your leader style is perhaps the clearest reflection of your beliefs and theology, note closely how you react to the chapters in this section. Style, stance, and strategy mirror your views of humankind and God.

(1) Leaders take three dimensions of leadership into account: the leader's preferred style, the style (or styles) of the followers, and the particular demands of each leadership situation. The unique mix of factors inherent in each leadership situation shapes the leader's response to and success with that specific pacesetting opportunity.

(2) Leaders balance mission and morale. Leaders encounter a wide range of leadership demands. Leaders are charged with helping the organization reach for its goals and with helping group members act confidently. Leaders deal in the future. Consequently, they try to use those leadership approaches that build people and structures for long-term effectiveness. They blend and balance the best features of both goal pursuit and interpersonal spirit into their basic leader style.

(3) Leaders maintain flexibility. Some organizational demands call for a primary emphasis on mission, production, and task-orientation. Other situations require a basic stress on morale, *esprit de corps*, and relationships. Like many professional baseball players, good leaders develop the flexibility to hit from both sides of home plate.

(4) Leaders serve their followers and their organizations. Real leaders conquer their power hunger and ambitions. They are willing to think of and serve their cause and community.

(5) Leaders work strategically. They choose their targets, focus their energies, determine what project takes the highest priority, delegate well, and work deliberately to create a new tomorrow.

CHAPTER VIII

Balancing People and Projects

(Catalysts/Nehemiah in Nehemiah 1-7)

Nehemiah was an extraordinarily well-balanced leader. He is remembered primarily as a construction project coordinator. In fact, he was much more. He was a builder of walls and of people.[1] Few leaders in the Bible did as well at managing tasks and relationships simultaneously. As a result, an enduring foundation was laid in both persons and places for the Jewish nation.

Blending Mission and Morale

The book of Nehemiah is a lay leader's diary. Leader Nehemiah's dramatic story begins in Persian captivity during the fifth century before Christ and describes a pivotal event: saving the Jewish community from disintegration. The account of the reconstruction of Jerusalem's walls, taken together with the stories in the book of Ezra about rebuilding the Temple and the renewal of worship, reminded the Jews of their roots, their everlasting debt to God, and their calling to serve as a redemptive minority amid the nations of the world.

Nehemiah may have been an exile, but he was a powerful captive. He had become the king's personal servant, secure and comfortable. Then his brother and a delegation from Jerusalem

reported the terrible condition of the city and its inhabitants.
Jerusalem's residents were endangered, and the city lay in ruins.
This deplorable state of affairs was a religious and community
disgrace to Nehemiah. His heart was broken; he was driven into
fasting and mournful prayer. As a result, Nehemiah became a man
with a mission.

> I confess the sins we Israelites, including myself and my
> father's house, have committed against you. We have acted
> very wickedly toward you. We have not obeyed the com-
> mands, decrees and laws you gave your servant Moses.
> Remember the instruction you gave your servant Moses,
> saying, If you are unfaithful, I will scatter you among the
> nations, but if you return to me and obey my commands, then
> even if your exiled people are at the farthest horizon, I will
> gather them from there and bring them to the place I have
> chosen as a dwelling for my Name (Nehemiah 1:6-9, *NIV*).

Prayer apparently didn't lessen Nehemiah's concerns, but it
may have increased his courage. Four months later when the king
inquired about the reason for his sad face, Nehemiah was ready
with an answer and boldly asked the king for three favors: could
he go home and rebuild his hometown (even though this basic
request meant the king would have to reverse a Persian edict),
would the king assure safe passage back to Jerusalem, and would
the king provide materials for the construction job? To Nehemiah's
pleased surprise, the king granted all his wishes. In addition, the
king sent a military escort along for the trip and somewhat later
appointed Nehemiah the governor of Jerusalem (Nehemiah 5:14
and 10:1).
     Upon arrival in Jerusalem, Nehemiah employed effective
leadership strategies before he undertook rebuilding the wall and
securing the city. First, he listened to the residents for three days,
perhaps an attempt to assess the morale level of the citizenry
(Nehemiah 2:11). Then, he secretly evaluated the extent of the

task (Nehemiah 2:12-16). Finally, he gathered the city's officials and—speaking as an insider, as "we"—described their common plight, challenged them to act swiftly, and identified some new spiritual and political resources for them (Nehemiah 2:17-18).

The result of this town meeting may lend a hint to the reason Nehemiah has been called the first city manager. Straightforwardly, they made a decision. "Let us start rebuilding" (Nehemiah 2:18, *NIV*), they replied. Urban renewal commenced.

Action followed their decision. Before opposition could dampen the spirits of the citizens, the work was organized and begun. Teams were assigned portions of the wall, and they fell to work. Amazingly, the breached wall was restored in seven and one-half weeks. But this successful construction project had more than its share of detractors. Outside enemies constantly mocked and criticized the project as well as harassed and threatened the people (Nehemiah 2:10, 19; 3:1-3, 7: 4:15; 6: 1-14). Fellow Jews feared reprisals and repeatedly questioned the plan (Nehemiah 4: 12). The workers themselves understandably wore down at about midpoint and despaired of clearing the rubble (Nehemiah 4:10). Eventually, what had begun as a construction project also became a military effort. In order to proceed successfully and to secure the far-flung work force, unusual precautions were taken by Nehemiah.

> Those who carried materials did their work with one hand and held a weapon in the other, and each of the builders wore his sword at this side as he worked. But the man who sounded the trumpet stayed with me (Nehemiah 4:17-18, *NIV*).

Guards were posted, and as the wall rose out of the rubble, workers slept with their work clothes on and with their weapons always at hand (Nehemiah 4:23).

In the end, the wall was rebuilt in fifty-two days.

> So the wall was completed on the twenty-fifth of Elul, in fifty-two days. When all our enemies heard about this, all the

surrounding nations were afraid and lost their self-confidence,
because they realized that this work had been done with the
help of God (Nehemiah 6: 16, *NIV*).

Then the wall was dedicated in a solemn ceremony and allegiance
to the Law renewed. Because of Nehemiah's leadership, not only
do we have the most recent history of God's people from the Old
Testament era, we have a worshipping community from whom
four hundred years later a Leader would emerge to fulfill this Law.

Mastering the Balancing Act of Leadership

Nehemiah offers us a positive example of leadership practice, be-
cause he balanced mission and morale. He helped Jerusalem's
residents rebuild the city wall: that's mission. He helped them
believe in themselves again: that's morale. Beneath and beyond it
all, Nehemiah enabled the Jewish people to awake their faith and
reorganize their community life around the Law. That's effective
leadership.
You and I lead most effectively when we challenge, inspire,
model, enable, and encourage others. That's the discovery of
Kouzes and Posner in The Leadership Challenge.[2] *Nehemiah*
consistently applied these five leadership practices to his work.
To clarify mission, he (1) challenged the process and (2) inspired
a shared vision. To heighten morale, he (3) enabled others to act
and (4) encouraged their hearts. Linking the mission and morale
dimensions of leadership in his own personality and example, he
(5) modeled the way for his followers. Note how the Kouzes and
Posner perspective matches Nehemiah's approach to leadership.
First, Nehemiah clarified mission by challenging the process.
He refused to accept the status quo. He could have said, "Why fret
about Jerusalem? I don't live there any more. I may be an exile,
but I have a good job. Why rock the boat?" Instead, Nehemiah
gained the king's aid and the support of Jerusalem's populace in

changing his world from what it was to what it could become. He confronted opposition. Nehemiah, typical of good leaders, looked for ways to change, innovate, and grow. He took the risk of making mistakes in order to enrich and advance the group's life.

Second, Nehemiah also clarified mission by inspiring a shared vision. He demonstrated passion for a cause and appealed to emotions when he presented the facts and called for a commitment to rebuild. Nehemiah envisioned an uplifting and ennobling future and enlisted others in implementing their common vision.

Third, Nehemiah heightened morale by enabling others to act. He organized special teams to tackle specific tasks. He assured the workers of physical security by arming and guarding them. Nehemiah was able to foster collaboration by promoting cooperative goals and building trust. He empowered people, allowing them to make decisions and providing them with resources as they carried out those commitments. Interestingly, Kouzes and Posner consider enablement the single most important leadership practice.

Fourth, Nehemiah also heightened morale by encouraging the hearts of his followers. He demonstrated how to stand up for a cause, how to regain momentum (Nehemiah 4:15), and how to shrug off insults. Strikingly, Nehemiah set a pattern by praying for direction and strength (Nehemiah 1:5-11; 2:4; 4:4-5; 5:19; 6:9 and 14). Nehemiah recognized that the success of any project is the result of individual contributions and that celebration and worship feed our inner lives.

Last, Nehemiah linked mission and morale by modeling the way. He mourned, fasted, prayed, and repented. But mostly he acted and risked and set the pace and blazed the trail. Unlike others, Nehemiah defended the poor (Nehemiah 5:1-13) and served the cause without personal gain (Nehemiah 5:14-19). His example demonstrated his bedrock values and commitments.

Keeping Mission and Morale in Balance

Wanted: Leaders who get the job done without sacrificing their followers.

Wanted: Leaders who support their followers without losing sight of their tasks.

Wanted: Leaders who can serve a cause without becoming self-serving.

Wanted: Leaders who can balance mission and morale so that God's kingdom is advanced.

* * * * *

CHAPTER IX

When the Buck Stops on Your Desk

(Commanders/Gideon in Judges 6-8)

Some leaders rise to prominence when times are difficult and followers are immature and unpredictable. Taking command in chaotic situations is always challenging. Gideon and the judges found the buck had stopped with them—unsought. They provided directive leadership for the infant nation during some of Israel's darkest hours.

Tough Times Test Good People!

The judges of Israel were leaders who served "between the times." The nation was still taking shape, and religious and political temptations were constants for the immature confederation. In fact, a pattern emerged. Sin, oppression, deliverance, and faithfulness recurred in a cycle as Israel alternately found and lost her way. The Scripture describes the pendulum's swings honestly, graphically, and tragically:

> . . . another generation grew up, who knew neither the Lord nor what he had done for Israel . . . They forsook the Lord, the God of their fathers, who had brought them out of Egypt . . . They provoked the Lord to anger . . . In his anger against

Israel the Lord handed them over to raiders who plundered
them . . . They were in great distress.

Then the Lord raised up judges, who saved them out of the
hands of these raiders. Yet they would not listen to their
judges but prostituted themselves to other gods and worshiped
them. Unlike their fathers, they quickly turned away from the
way in which their fathers walked, the way of obedience to the
Lord's commands. Whenever the Lord raised up a judge for
them, he was with the judge and saved them out of the hands
of their enemies as long as the judge lived . . . But when the
judge died, the people returned to ways even more corrupt
than those of their fathers . . . They refused to give up their
evil practices and stubborn ways (Judges 2:10-19, *NIV*)

For roughly two hundred years, the judges functioned as local
military heroes and heroines. They rose up to confront a specific
crisis, served as rescuers temporarily, and then, like Gideon, returned to their pre-military lives (Judges 8:22-35). There were
only a half-dozen or so major judges and as many minor ones.
Some probably even served overlapping tours of duty. During
these Dark Ages of Israel's history the brave judges, never para-
gons of virtue anyway, delivered the nation from her oppressors by
battle, assassination, and revenge. Some of these judges had more
charisma than character. Still they were effective leaders for such
extreme circumstances, although they weren't exactly the good
guys in white hats every day of their lives. For example, Jephthah
was a near-bandit, and Samson was a charming rogue with extraordinary strength. To his credit, Gideon at least undertook his military stint with a sense of divine calling.

Gideon was one of the best known of the judges. He stepped
forward after seven years of raids and ravages to repel the camel-
mounted Midianites. Israel had turned back to God and begged for
a tough savior. But Gideon saw himself as a farmer rather than a
general. The conversation between God's messenger and Gideon
at the time of Gideon's call disclosed a lot about Israel's plight and

Gideon's level of confidence. Note how the state of Israel was
described, how God kept reassuring his judge, and how Gideon
continued to request guarantees:

> Messenger: "The Lord is with you, mighty warrior."
> Gideon: ". . . now the Lord has abandoned us . . ."
> Messenger: "Go in the strength you have and save Israel . . ."
> Gideon: ". . . how can I save Israel? My clan is the weakest in
> Manasseh, and I am the least in my family."
> Messenger: "I will be with you . . ."
> Gideon: ". . . give me a sign . . ."
> Messenger: "Tear down your father's altar to Baal . . . build a
> proper kind of altar to the Lord your God . . ."
> Gideon: "If you will save Israel by my hand as you have
> promised . . . Allow me one more test . . ."
> (Judges 6:12-39, *NIV*).

Finally, Gideon accepted the rescue responsibility. Then God
surprised him with an observation that the smaller Israel's army,
the better the result would be. Although the foe had marshalled a
large force, Israel's 32,000 soldiers were seen by God as too many.
If Israel should prevail, they might assume they had won the war
without God's help (Judges 7:2). The solution was simple. Ask
who's afraid and send those soldiers home. Twenty-two thousand
men "volunteered" to go back home. Still God felt another reduc-
tion in force campaign was needed. In this test, only the 300
fighters who drank alertly were kept for the key battles (Judges 7:
4-7).

Now the Israelites were ready to go to war. Almost. Gideon
used the cover of darkness to spy out the Midianite camp. To his
surprise and comfort, he discovered the soldiers of Midian feared
"the sword of Gideon . . . God has given the Midianites and the
whole camp into his hands" (Judges 7:14, *NIV*). The story of the
panicked rout triggered by trumpets, torches, and smashed water
pots is known to every child or adult who has attended Sunday

School (Judges 7:15-21). The Midianites were chased and defeated. Gideon tortured the elders of Succoth and avenged the deaths of his brothers by personally executing two leaders (Judges 8:4-21). The blush of victory didn't last long, however.

So dependent were the Israelites that they tried to make Gideon their king. He refused with good theological judgment: "The Lord will rule over you" (Judges 8:23, *NIV*). Although Israel continued at peace for the remaining forty years of Gideon's life, Gideon was haunted by one action he took. He used the Midianite booty to make a worship vestment that he displayed at his hometown. The outcome? "All Israel prostituted themselves by worshiping (the vestment) there, and it became a snare to Gideon and his family" (Judges 8:27, *NIV*). Dependent followers are always vulnerable to leaders whose own psychological needs seduce them into unhealthy tactics by their own lack of judgment.

When Directive Leaders Are Required

Two situations—chaos or instability and inertia or overstability— call for directive leaders like the judges. In either case, direct action is required if the organization is to become effective. Both unstable and overstable situations respond to someone who seizes the moment and acts boldly. That's the style of the Commander leader.[1]

Chaos can be stabilized by leaders who structure the situation by initiative and calm the unrest by personal impact. This fact is noted in the era of the judges. When God raised up a judge, Israel found its moorings—as long as the judge was on the scene. When the judge was gone, apostasy and chaos recurred.

Inertia can be confronted by Commanders too. When organizational life has ground to a halt, directive leaders can bump the institution enough to move it off dead center and regain some momentum. If an organization has drifted into an "at ease in

Zion" posture, such nudging of the institution will be uncomfortable for those who have found a certain peace in inertia.

Commander or directive leaders prefer mission over morale and production over persons. That's their bias and their strength. They "get the job done" although sometimes they hurt feelings or even sacrifice relationships in the bargain. As one pastor reported, "I had to sacrifice 700 members to save this church!" Whatever else could be said about his leadership approach, his Commander style was obvious. Wess Roberts claims . . ."your greatness will be made possible through the extremes of your personality—the very extremes that sometimes make for campfire satire and legendary stories."

Not all Commanders are so heavy-handed, however. One subtype described as Benevolent Dictators exude warmth to disguise their demanding and inflexible side. Even so, Commanders commonly keep so much pressure on their followers that they invite resistance or even rebellion. In his Leadership Secrets of Attila the Hun, *Wess Roberts "quotes" Attila on his reputation as "the scrouge of God": Itisn't easy being the Scourge of God, but it has its advantages in dealing with the enemy."[2] Commenting further on the respect a leader needs, Roberts observes:*

> *When deference is born of fear, however, it results in an unwillingness to serve and becomes manifested as passive resistance to authority and purpose. It further leads to subversion, to sabotage and to generally low morale among those you are attempting to lead.[3]*

Directive leadership, taken to its extreme, ceases to be leadership and deteriorates into "power wielding."[4] Power wielders tend to be overcome by ambition and lose sight of their followers' needs and interests. Hitler is one political example of the directive personality gone awry. The church could offer its pantheon of power wielders too, by the way.

Commanders have their times, places, and zones of effective-

ness. They lead best when an emergency state exists. Therefore, their style fits short-term circumstances best. Fortunately for organizations, emergencies are ordinarily brief. Unfortunately for some directive leaders, they may fall into the "task first, last, and always" rut and become unable to adjust to new situations and needs. Tragically, some directive leaders operate so comfortably amid chaos that they become addicted to the ragged edge and create unrest in order to come to their organization's rescue. Sad to say, the crisis they hunger to command is the crisis they created.

Giving Directive Leaders Their Due

Wanted: Leaders who are willing to take charge—even reluctantly—during crises and tough times.

Wanted: Leaders who are able to be directive when situations call for it but who refuse to use situations for their own purposes or abuse their followers.

Wanted: Leaders who step forward during emergencies and then step aside when their gifts no longer fit the circumstance, who know when to hold and when to fold.

Wanted: Leaders who realize an unwilling dictator is to be preferred over an eager power wielder.

Wanted: Leaders who realize the risks of leadership include the possibility that the buck may stop on their desks.

*   *   *   *   *

CHAPTER X

When You Need the Benefit of the Doubt

(Encouragers/Barnabas in Acts 11-15)

Barnabas, nicknamed "Son of Encouragement" (Acts 4:36, *NIV*), had a consistent track record of offering the benefit of the doubt to a broad array of people. He was an Encourager leader *par excellence*.

I Need a Second Chance!

It was a short prayer. Ordinarily, the dedicatory prayer at the inauguration of the new leader of a major religious institution merits a longer, a more elaborate, and, frankly, a more "religious" petition to the Almighty. But, the circumstances were a bit unusual because the pray-er was a layman, a man who had spent his life working with his hands rather than with words, and the honoree's father. Although the pomp of the high and holy occasion was somewhat intimidating, the pray-er didn't lose his perspective or earthy wisdom. "Lord," he prayed in a single sentence, "give my son the benefit of the doubt."

The benefit of the doubt. Each of us needs a second chance sooner or later. We all need the benefit of the doubt. That's why we appreciate leaders who bless us by giving the benefit of the doubt and offering second chances. Barnabas was such a leader.

He blessed those whom he touched through his ministry of encouragement.

Barnabas appears in five separate New Testament incidents. In each of them, he gave others the benefit of the doubt. The needy, turncoats, pioneers, theologians, and quitters all received second chances from Encourager Barnabas.

The first time Barnabas appears in the pages of the New Testament he comes to the aid of needy Christians in Jerusalem. He sells some land and donates the proceeds to the church's treasury for the use of all (Acts 4:36-37). That's encouragement.

The next appearance of Barnabas showcases his ability to see potential in others and to sponsor them. Saul, newly converted, finds himself in a crossfire. He's facing murder by the Jews on the one hand and exclusion by the believers in Christ on the other (Acts 9:19b-26). Turncoats are typically hated by those they've abandoned and distrusted by those they're trying to join. Into this turmoil stepped Barnabas. He vouched for Saul's conversion and preaching ministry (Acts 9:27-28). He gave Saul an open door into the believing community. That's the benefit of the doubt—and this courtesy changed the Christian movement forever.

A third episode about Barnabas is of special interest to leaders. When persecution scattered Christ's followers beyond their original home base, a church flourished in Antioch. The Jerusalem believers dispatched Barnabas to Antioch to help out.

> . . . they sent Barnabas to Antioch. When he arrived and saw the evidence of the grace of God, he was glad and encouraged them all to remain true to the Lord with all their hearts (Acts 11:22b-23, *NIV*).

Rather than pressure the Antioch church as a quality control expert from the home office in Jerusalem, Barnabas simply encouraged them to revel in grace and follow Christ wholeheartedly. Later, when he had apparently done all he could to stabilize the Antioch congregation, he called in Paul as a consultant and teacher.

The result? "The disciples were called Christians first at Antioch" (Acts 11:26, *NIV*). Even pioneers need the benefit of the doubt at times.

The first missionary journey yielded a fourth telling vignette. Young John Mark, Barnabas' relative, dropped out on the first tour (Acts 13:13). When the second evangelistic trip was being planned, Barnabas nominated John Mark, the quitter, for the team again. Paul heatedly resisted, and the Paul and Barnabas alliance ended in a "sharp disagreement" (Acts 15:30a, *NIV*). Significantly, Barnabas gave John Mark another chance at missionary work and mentored him into leadership effectiveness (Acts 15:39b).

Pause for a moment and consider how significant Barnabas' penchant for the second chance was to the Christian movement. He gave both Paul and Mark a new lease on faith. Paul is credited with nearly one-half of the New Testament. Mark wrote the earliest Gospel, the book that Matthew and Luke are both based on and from which they quote heavily. Think of it! Taken together, Paul and Mark produced roughly two-thirds of the New Testament record. All because Barnabas believed in giving folks a second chance!

Lastly, the Jerusalem Council provided an early theological watershed for the growing Christian movement. Two groups faced each other. The "Then Party" argued that believers needed to become Jews first and then they could qualify to become Christians. (At times, even theologians need the benefit of the doubt.) The "Only Party" claimed only grace was needed to belong to Christ. The testimonies of Barnabas and Paul tilted the scales toward the grace only perspective, carried the day, and shaped the basic beliefs of the early church (Acts 15:12). James summed up the outcome: "It is my judgment, therefore, that we should not make it difficult for the Gentiles who are turning to God" (Acts 15:19, *NIV*).

In conclusion, the pattern is obvious and clear. Every time Barnabas leaves his footprints on the pages of the New Testament he's extending the benefit of the doubt to some soul. He lived up to his nickname, the Encourager. That's an especially effective leader style for people-oriented situations.

Encouragers: When Morale Is the Issue

Encourager leaders[1] are empathic types who stress peoples' needs more than production quotas and emphasize morale over mission. In other words, these leaders are tilted toward a relational approach to problem-solving. Consequently, they fit some leadership situations better than others.

Encouragers are people-persons. They pour oil on troubled waters, hold hands, pat heads, listen well, soothe hurt feelings, mediate differences, develop fellowship, and bind people together. Encouragers see potential and possibilities, think the best, and give others the benefit of the doubt. Barnabas and the Encourager leader style fit each other like a hand and glove.

Although Barnabas was an effective missionary and could be task-oriented, his best gift was blessing others through encouragement. He was what Deal and Kennedy in Corporate Cultures *call a "compass-hero."[2] These heroes inspire others daily during times of turbulence and change. Compass-heroes are role models who point out the new direction by setting the pace, using their special skills well, and symbolizing the needed changes. They model the way. Barnabas caught the front edge of the new faith wave we call Christianity. Leading during this era of radical change, Barnabas stabilized congregations, reclaimed persons, and helped the young movement solidify its faith. He was a living compass while the new faith was trying to get its bearings.*

Like a priest in a church, there are organizational priests too.[3] These key leaders keep the flock together. They listen to confessions. They help solve problems. They bandage the wounded, ease the frustrated souls, and give hope to the discouraged. Frequently, they move behind the scenes and operate in staff positions. Priests are therefore often more powerful than visible. Isn't it interesting that Barnabas was Paul's sponsor on Acts 9 and 11 but by Acts 13 the order of the names switched to Paul first and Barnabas last? Barnabas the leader had became Barnabas the follower. There's no hint that he was upset over losing the limelight. That's typical of the organizational priest. He or she moves easily throughout the group caring for others with little or no need to seize center stage. These team players can lead or follow, but they rarely lose influence. They consistently offer the benefit of the doubt to their fellows.

When organizations move into periods of stress or conflict, Encouragers lead well. They point the way like a compass and care for the group like a priest. Barnabas led the young church when it was finding its identity, developing its leaders, and defining its beliefs. The emerging church needed the benefit of the doubt on occasion, and many of its members needed second chances in their lives. Barnabas was an effective encouraging leader for such a time.

Looking for Encouragers

Wanted: Leaders who have a heart for broken followers and who have the patience to make the necessary repairs.

Wanted: Leaders who can provide discipline as well as the benefit of the doubt—and know when each is appropriate.

Wanted: Leaders who can spot future leaders and develop potential into reality.

Wanted: Leaders who are morale builders, fellowship enrichers, and organizational priests.

Wanted: Leaders who are compass-heroes, who know Him who is True North.

Wanted: Leaders who can move into follower roles without ego explosions.

* * * * *

CHAPTER XI

Burning Out from Bossiness

(Flexibility/Moses in Exodus 18)

Moses learned to adjust his leadership style by trial and error. It was almost a costly lesson.

Pressure Cooker in the Corner Office

Visits from in-laws rarely go unnoticed. But this was not a casual, ordinary social call. There was an agenda for this trip, and that agenda demanded a serious, heart-to-heart talk between father-in-law and son-in-law. It wouldn't necessarily be an easy conversation. After all, Moses had become a famous leader, a fact his father-in-law hadn't exactly missed. Everyone had seen the mighty acts God had done in delivering the Hebrews from slave labor in Egypt. Everyone also recognized Moses as a person especially blessed by God (Exodus 18:1). But Jethro, Moses' father-in-law, had more on his mind than a congratulatory greeting and a backyard barbecue. Jethro had enjoyed just about enough of Moses' success. It was time to capture this whirlwind who was his son-in-law for a serious conversation.

Moses had been busy. That was part of the problem Jethro wanted to confront. For a man who had spent a major portion of his life in the quiet isolation of the desert, Moses had seen more than his fair share of fast-moving history. His life had begun during turbulent times, a time when boy babies were to be drowned in the Nile by order of Pharoah. Moses' life had been saved in that famous Bible story recalled in somewhat garbled form by Huck Finn as involving Moses and "the bullrushers." The highlights of Moses' life must have flashed before his eyes in a rush at times. Raised a prince. Self-exiled because of a murder. Called by God at the burning bush. Spokesperson for God in the plagues upon Egypt. Survivor of the Passover. Leader of the Exodus. Fed by quail and manna. Winner of battles. Moses' life was becoming a Horatio Alger success story (Exodus 1-17).

But success had exacted a price. Moses had felt the pressure of executive leadership and had been forced to farm his family out to his in-laws (Exodus 18:2-4). And that was the agenda Jethro brought with him from Midian (Exodus 18:5-6).

You have to admire Jethro's style. It must have been a temptation to have his say and nail this lopsided leader to the wall. Jethro could have said:

> Son, it's good to see you and share your success. As you can see, I've brought your wife and sons home to you. The wife and I have enjoyed having them with us the last several months. But—and let me be frank here—I've had about as much of your children as I can stand. I know you've been overwhelmed with this Exodus thing, but enough is enough. I've brought your family home to you. While you're becoming the Father of your Country, become the father of your children and the husband of your wife!

Jethro may have readied his speech. (And Moses may have felt his guilt.) But Jethro was wiser than that. Rather than plunge into a heavy-handed lecture on family responsibilities, Jethro chose a consultative role. First, he relaxed in Moses' tent and heard the tales of triumph about Egypt and the Exodus (Exodus 18:7-8). Jethro then praised God's rescuing actions, worshipped, and sat with the tribal elders at dinner (Exodus 18:9-12). Finally, he

watched Moses work, asked strategic questions about Moses'
motives and style, and made a proposal about how to avoid the
inevitable burnout looming ahead for Moses (Exodus 18:13-23):
"What you are doing is not good. You and these people who come
to you will only wear yourselves out. The work is too heavy for
you; you cannot handle it alone" (Exodus 18:18, *NIV*).

To his credit, Moses took Jethro's advice and changed his
leader style from the do-everything-by-myself director to a man-
age-by-exception delegator (Exodus 18:24-26). In the end, Jethro
went back home—alone, happy, and maybe already anticipating a
bit the next, much briefer, visit with his grandchildren, daughter,
and his famous son-in-law (Exodus 18:27).

The Consequences of Leader Style

*Every leader style has its predictable outcome. Moses was begin-
ning to learn his leader style lesson. He had adopted or fallen into
a Commander leadership style.[1] Commanders take the exclusive
burden of leadership on their shoulders. They exercise authority
comfortably because they may see themselves standing between
God and their followers. Having God's ear makes for a lean and
clean leadership situation for Commanders: "I know and I tell
you what and when; you hear and you do what I say or leave."*

*Commanders often mistake the rescuing actions of God for
their own powers and try to rescue everyone and every situation.
That over-reaching style leads to inevitable burnout for leaders
and eventual pressure or conflict for their followers. As one wag
notes about Moses the workaholic, "The Hebrews wouldn't have
wandered in the wilderness for forty years if Moses had only asked
directions!" But, the Commander has to do it all himself.*

*Commanders work well in emergency situations. Moses had
responded correctly. What is more volatile than trying to forge a
ragtag bunch of slave tribes into a new nation? What's more of an
emergency than having your back to the sea while the entire*

Egyptian army charges down upon you with swords drawn? What's more of a crisis than having the folks you just rescued grumble about their freedom and wish for slavery again? New, unstructured, and chaotic circumstances respond to Commanders, those leaders who provide comforting structure for their followers and add necessary structure to the organizational situation.[2] Moses had read his past leadership situation well. A Commander can, after all, lead a forced march.

Fortunately, life is rarely an ongoing crisis. Unfortunately, leaders may get stuck in the style they've gotten used to. But, when the situation changes, their familiar style no longer fits. Frequently, they simply try harder to make the old, habitual methods work. In Moses' case, he found that style has consequences. Moses was on the verge of experiencing the burnout of bossiness. In particular, he discovered that Commanders get worn down by the weight of their over-responsible streak. And they get seduced by their need to be needed and to keep their followers dependent on them. So the Commander style of leadership, which works well as a short-term approach to crisis management, eventually erodes leaders' resources and cheats their followers from growing into leaders by keeping them in perpetual immaturity.

Moses accepted Jethro's suggestion and took on a Catalyst style of leadership. He realized the Commander of an Exodus had to adjust into the Catalyst of a nation. He learned to select and develop other leaders. He began to delegate. He concentrated on the exceptional, difficult decisions. And maybe he played catch with his sons. As a leader, Moses began to act like a Catalyst, think of the future, and invest his energies strategically. Moses must have realized that the same God who had met him at the burning bush and beyond would lead the Hebrews into an exciting, new era of adventure with Moses at the helm—if Moses could expand his leader style for a changing challenge.

Growing Up as a Leader

Wanted: Leaders who understand the demands of leadership situations and organizational cycles and adjust wisely to act directively in crises and catalytically for the long-term.

Wanted: Leaders who can see the consequences—for themselves and their followers—of their leader styles.

Wanted: Leaders who realize that professional style has personal impacts on health and family.

Wanted: Leaders who never forget how to learn.

Wanted: Leaders whose styles are not determined by ego needs.

Wanted: Leaders whose faith remembers God's work in the past.

* * * * *

CHAPTER XII

Are Good Guys Wimps?

(Servanthood/Jesus in Mark 10:5-45)

Servant. The word smacks of bowing down to others, taking on
unpopular jobs, and knuckling under. For some, servanthood
describes meekness, if not outright weakness. But Jesus gave a
new definition to servanthood. He demonstrated a new insight for
leaders: servants do not think less of themselves, but they do think
of themselves less.

The Source of Greatness

James and John, those mercurial sons of thunder, took the plunge.
They got their bids in early. Jesus had just given the most detailed,
graphic, and definite forecast of his betrayal and death that he had
yet shared with his followers. Astonishment, fear, and foreboding
were overpowering among them. Time was short. Now, they
thought, was the time to act—and to ask.

   "Teacher," they requested, "when the kingdom comes, we
would like important jobs. Could one of us be your vice-president
and the other your secretary of state?" (Mark 10:37). Whether
buoyed by blind ambition or basking amid a sense of entitlement
and perceived superiority growing out of family affluence (Mark
1:20), at least these two brothers had no doubt about the ultimate

triumph of Jesus. Adopting a strategy similar to the Confederate commander who preferred to be "firstest with the mostest," James and John pushed to the front of the line and dared to ask for prominence. If nothing's ventured, then nothing's gained, they reasoned. So they went out on the limb.

Their inquiry drew two intense responses. The other ten apostles were outraged (Mark 10:41). "What's the big idea? The nerve of you guys! How could you two ask such a thing?" wondered the less aggressive ten. Were they indignant because they had wanted to ask for prominent places too but had feared taking the risk? Were they embarrassed because they had realized too late that they had missed an opportunity for advancement? Did they envy James and John's timing, sensing that they had been outflanked? We could make a better guess if we knew who told the ten what had happened and how they "heard about this" (Mark 10:41, *NIV*). In any event, the other ten apostles were extremely angry with James and John.

The other intriguing response came directly from Jesus. "Do you think you're up to the job? Can you drink my cup and join in my kind of baptism?" pressed Jesus. "Sure," they quickly agreed. "Okay," Jesus granted, "The cup and baptism are yours." In spite of the ominous echo of martyrdom, James and John must have thought they had pulled off a coup. Then, a surprising statement left them stunned, unsure and empty. Jesus added, "The top spots in the kingdom are another matter. Those places "belong to those for whom they have been prepared" (Mark 10:38-40, *NIV*). "Wait a minute," they wondered, "If the prominent posts aren't Jesus' to give, how can we land them?"

Before James and John could probe the answer to their question and before the angry ten could arm themselves with tar and feathers, Jesus summoned all twelve into a huddle for the most profound statement he would make about the nature of Christian leadership. He drew a sharp contrast and then spelled out the cost of leadership.

You know that
those who are regarded as rulers of the Gentiles
lord it over them,
and their high officials
exercise authority over them.
Not so with you.
Instead, whoever wants to become great among you
must be your servant,
and whoever wants to be first
must be slave of all.
For even the Son of Man did not come to be served,
but to serve,
and to give his life as a ransom for many"
(Mark 10:42-45, *NIV*).

Ouch! There it was. Become a servant instead of being a boss—that was Jesus' philosophy. Whatever became of titles, perks, and corner offices? Jesus' idea was revolutionary and un-expected. He had turned the traditional organizational pyramid upside down! No boss—and certainly no bully—at the pinnacle. No orders. No imperialistic attitude. No superiority. This ap-proach startled the apostles into self-debate. Who wanted to work in behalf of the group? Who wanted leaders who were servants? Each pondered, "Did I hear him correctly?" Suddenly the top jobs in Jesus' kingdom sounded far less prestigious and much more costly. Jesus had gotten their full attention; he had set a new standard of greatness. They asked, "Mind if we take a little time and think this whole matter through?" They were about to learn that servant leaders think no less of themselves, but they may think of themselves less.

Servanthood as a Leader Stance

Servanthood is more a stance for leadership than a style or a strategy. A stance provides a foundational place to stand, a basic outlook, and a set of values to live out. Stance precedes style, your pattern of action, as well as your strategy, priorities, and sense of timing for leadership. Stance is the seedbed for style and strategy's roots. Servanthood, then, is better seen as a leadership stance than a leader style or strategy. Rather than standing over others, servant leaders stand alongside, stand with, and are willing to stand under their followers.

Servanthood permeates the biblical message. God called the ancestors of Abraham to be blessings to the world (Genesis 12:2). Israel was to be a servant nation (Isaiah 42, 49, 50, 52, and 53.) Jesus took up a towel and a basin in order to serve his followers (John 13:16). It's no surprise, then, that the hymn fragment expressing the loftiest Christology in the New Testament reminds us that Jesus took on "the very nature of a servant" (Philippians 2:7, NIV).

It's instructive that the servant leader emphasis follows on the heels of a reference to Jesus' passion. He served humankind at the cross as well as at the baptismal font, on the Mount of Transfiguration, with the towel and basin, and from the empty tomb. Hear the leadership questions from these events:

—Servant of the Baptismal: Am I willing to be identified with this cause and this community?

—Servant of the Mountaintop: Am I willing to share the peaks and valleys of this community for this cause?

—Servant of the Towel and Basin: Am I willing to do menial tasks to sustain this cause and this community?

—Servant of the Cross: Am I willing to sacrifice for this cause and this community?

—Servant of the Empty Tomb: Am I willing to demonstrate the staying power of this cause and this community?

Note the continuing themes of cause and community that act as stabilizers for servants.

Robert K. Greenleaf, writing from a layperson's perspective in his Servant Leadership,[1] *describes servanthood in demanding terms. Savor these snapshots of servant leaders. Enrich others by their presence. Become goal-oriented dreamers. Live by the better idea—within community. Concentrate on one thing at a time. Live to act, initiate, risk, structure. Build people first. Develop into healers. Use power to create opportunities. Lead by searching, listening first, conceptualizing, and trying to understand. Become intuitive, aware, alert, intense, accepting, empathic, and persuasive. Lead as servants and, consequently, follow only servant leaders.*

In one sense, servant leadership is practicing the Golden Rule in the workplace. This approach has been used successfully in the American marketplace by James Cash Penney. J. C. Penney expanded a small general merchandise store opened in Kemmerer, Wyoming in 1902 into a business empire on one principle: treating customers the way he wanted to be treated himself. No wonder Penney's were called The Golden Rule Stores. Penney applied the Golden Rule to his relationship with his employees, too. He called them associates and treated them as partners. That's how he wanted to be treated himself.

Ernest Mosley, a prominent Baptist leader, in a recent lecture commented on Jesus' washing the apostles' feet. He specified four ways servant leaders can "lead with a towel" in their treatment of their followers:

wipe the dirt from others' feet—*with a word of encouragement or an expression of genuine concern;*

wipe the tears from others' eyes—*by being sensitive to others' disappointments, losses, and sorrows;*

wipe the egg from others' faces—*through restoring persons after failures, humiliations, or mistakes;*

wipe away the temptation to throw in the towel—*in the face of personal and prfessional disappointments and obstacles in leadership.*

Mosley's poetic depiction of servant leadership reminds us powerfully that servanthood is a stance of strength. Wimps and weaklings need not apply for servant leader positions.

Wade Paris, a Baptist pastor in Kansas City, tells a wonderful story from his childhood about servanthood. "We kids made fun of Dr. Sanders in McNairy County, Tennessee. Doc wore old clothes and prayed long public prayers. He lived in a very simple house. One day I made an unkind remark about Doc. My dad said, 'Son, I don't think you understand Doc.' 'How's that?' 'Well, Doc is really a wealthy man.' That was a surprise to me. 'When he was younger he served as a country doctor, literally wearing out his health for his patients. He always lived frugally. But he gave generously to others and his church. He paid for much of his church's building though few people know it. And Doc has paid college tuition for many young people who otherwise couldn't go.' I was ashamed. Doc was living like Jesus and I was making fun of him. But so it is with true Christians and the world."

Doc's real "strength" was his "weakness." In Wade's mind, Doc Sanders leapfrogged from last to first in one simple story of service. That leap of faith to servanthood was Jesus' radical challenge for James and John as well as today's leaders. Only the strong can serve. Only strength allows servant leaders to think of themselves less while not thinking less of themselves.

Serving from Strength

Wanted: Leaders who think of themselves less but don't think less of themselves.

Wanted: Leaders who emerge out of the mainstream of their groups because they have served the group well.

Wanted: Leaders who concentrate on aligning their organization's and their follower's needs.

Wanted: Leaders who are more sensitive to Lordship than they are hungry for overlordship.

Wanted: Leaders who distinguish between authority and power, who realize authority is linked to their organizational role while power grows out of personal and professional service.

* * * * *

CHAPTER XIII

Pursuing the Most Important — First, Last, Always

(Strategy/Paul in Acts 13-19)

The Bible reminds leaders to note the fullness of time (Mark 1:15), to count the cost (Luke 14:28), and to reap those fields that are ripe and ready for harvesting (John 4:35). Like Esther, we are alerted that we may have risen to our place of leadership "for such a time as this" (Esther 4:14, *NIV*). These images in the Bible call on leaders to become strategic thinkers. In this quality, we are following the nature of God, the master strategist of humanity's redemption. Paul practiced strategy in his missionary work.

Strategy—Generalship for Goal Seeking

Strategy, from a Greek word for generalship, is the art of devising and employing plans toward a goal. Strategy is necessary because there are rarely more than enough resources to go around. Leaders, then, recognize that we can only plan for the opportunities we can identify and only plan with the resources we can command.

Paul, the missionary, was a canny strategist. To extend God's kingdom, Paul locked in on an anchoring goal, identified a few key result areas, selected the most important of all his goals, concentrated on reaching responsive audiences and high profile geographic regions, and focused his energies and resources on a generally preselected sequence of actions. The six panels or sections of the book of Acts, telling the story of the victors and victories of first generation Christianity's expansion of its influence across the Roman Empire, provide a clear case history of strategy development.

Note just five of the illustrative strategy choices Paul applied to the expansion of Christianity. (1) He appealed initially to persons who already had a religious background before he reached out to those without faith. He began in worship centers, used the familiar Scriptures, and explained the continuity in God's redemptive plan:

> We tell you the good news: What God promised our fathers he has fulfilled for us, their children, by raising up Jesus . . . Therefore, my brothers, I want you to know that through Jesus the forgiveness of sins is proclaimed to you . . . When the congregation was dismissed, many of the Jews and devout converts to Judaism followed Paul and Barnabas, who talked with them and urged them to continue in the grace of God (Acts 13:32-43, *NIV*).

(2) He stabilized the new churches he started:

> . . . they returned to Lystra, Iconium, and Antioch, strengthening the disciples and encouraging them to remain true to the faith . . . Paul and Barnabas appointed elders . . . (Acts 14:21-23, *NIV*).

Not only did he want to preserve his efforts, he wanted to use these base camps as launch pads for future expansion. (3) He freed faith from religion in the Jerusalem Council's debates over the basic character of Christianity in Acts 15. (4) He made a strategic decision and chose to evangelize the West (Acts 16:6-10).

(5) He used many methods to proclaim one central message. Take note of only one method—the ministry arenas—Paul se-

lected. For example, in Philippi, Paul preached by the riverside and in prison (Acts 16). In Thessalonica, Paul preached in the synagogue, precipitating mob reaction (Acts 17:1-9). In Berea, Paul conducted thorough Bible studies in the synagogue (Acts 17:10-15). In Athens, Paul dialogued with the philosophers (Acts 17:16-34) and, in Ephesus, he led daily discussions in a public lecture hall for two years (Acts 19:8-19). In Corinth, Paul set up an alternate worship center (Acts 18:1-8). In other words, Paul sought out and concentrated on those ministry arenas in which the message of the kingdom of God received the most favorable hearing.

Notice that Paul adjusted his methodologies to his audiences and opportunities. His basic message and objectives remained constant, however. That's strategic thinking at its best.

Choosing the Best

The Marines claim they want a few good men. I assume they mean they want to recruit only the best fighters. In other words, they intend to work strategically in their enlistment efforts.

To work strategically requires leaders first to think strategically. Unfortunately, there is no School of Strategic Thinking per se. But there are some ingredients in expanding our strategic thinking capabilities. We can choose visionary mentors.[1] We can hone our own personal sense of mission and direction. We can cut back on defensive living, on "looking at the ground for snakes," and begin scanning horizons. We can get training in planning skills. In other words, we can do our best to focus on doing the right thing at the right time for the right result. That's strategic thinking.

Let's contrast leaders who practice strategic thinking with those who try to practice risk-free acting:

(1) Strategic thinkers are effective and do the right things; risk-free actors are efficient and do things right.

(2) Strategic thinkers are success-oriented, take the offense, and are willing to take risks; risk-free actors are geared toward playing safe defense, avoiding failure, and doing damage control.

(3) Strategic thinkers are proactive but are able to delay gratification to order to achieve the right result; risk-free actors are reactive and want to see immediate outcomes.

(4) Strategic thinkers are an innovative and flexible minority; risk-free actors are a traditional and static majority.

(5) Strategic thinkers look at the world through telescopes and wide-angle lens; risk-free actors view the world in microscopic perspective.

(6) Strategic thinkers are change-explorers, are improvement-oriented, are able to work patiently for incremental change, and use multiple approaches in change management; risk-free actors prefer the status quo, are all-or-nothing adjustors, and tend to get locked in on a single method of change management.

(7) Strategic thinkers are self-aware, secure personalities who relate to others in direct, covenantal fashion; risk-free actors are more survival-oriented persons who relate to others on an "as needed" basis.

(8) Strategic thinkers focus on mission and morale by identifying key result areas or those initiatives in which we must succeed if we're to achieve our basic purpose; risk-free actors try to keep their noses clean, stay out of the line of fire, and, thereby, may misinterpret safety for success.

Strategic thinking has an inherently religious flavor. Religious leaders practice faith, a near synonym for risk. They also fix their action compasses on bedrock goals and values. Those who attempt to lead from a risk-free perspective actually risk losing both their ability to do the right action at the right time for the right goal as well as their opportunity for "faith-ing." Strategic thinking is, in the final analysis, an act of faith.

Only the Basic, the First, the Best

Wanted: Leaders who concentrate on taking the right action at the right time for the right result.

Wanted: Leaders who can see open doors of potential and opportunity.

Wanted: Leaders who have the will to select the few "best" options from among the many "good" alternatives.

Wanted: Leaders who identify those key result areas of greatest impact and significance—and act on them.

Wanted: Leaders who are willing to think strategically before acting strategically.

Wanted: Leaders who apply faith to opportunity.

* * * * *

Tensions: How Do Great Leaders Act Amid Conflict?

Have you ever noticed that a group of four people usually contains at least five opinions? Opinion overload tenses up leaders and groups alike. Strongly held, diverse points of view strain nerves and relationships. In spite of the discomfort, tension is part and parcel of leadership. Conflict comes with the territory of leadership. Great leaders learn to deal with the natural tensions and conflicts of pacesetting—if they are to be effective.

Tension. It's a word that knots leaders' stomachs. Tension suggests pressure, friction, contention, strife, discord, and hostility. That's not very good news for leaders who are harmony-seekers! Yet, effective leaders resolve tensions and conflicts—in persons and organizations, between supervisors and supervisees, and in failure as well as in success.

This section of four chapters recognizes several basic leadership actions:

- Leaders act to escalate conflict strategically when foundational religious values have been perverted.
- Leaders act as peacemakers in their groups and organizations.
- Leaders act with integrity under bad supervision and learn to supervise well.
- Leaders act to recover perspective when they fail—and to keep their perspective when they succeed.

A cluster of leadership themes runs throughout the chapters of this section:

(1) Leaders stay clear enough about their core values and principles to know what to confront and what to let pass as well as when to escalate conflict and when to walk away. They know when to hold and call as well as when to fold and cash in their chips.

(2) Leaders function as peacemakers. Peacemaking is bedrock religious leadership. But reconciliation and peacemaking aren't the same thing. Leaders try to make peace; only God reconciles and turns enemies into friends.

(3) Leaders supervise with caring consistency when in charge and practice the Golden Rule when following. The balance is crucial because all leaders follow at times and all followers lead at points.

(4) Leaders risk and therefore fail. Great leaders make comebacks and therefore win. It's important to remember that neither victory nor defeat is permanent; both winning and losing have their special lessons to teach leaders.

CHAPTER XIV

What's Worth Losing Your Cool Over?

(Escalation/Jesus in Mark 3:1-6 and Matthew 21:10-17)

Leadership increases in importance when conflicting values collide. Some conflicts cannot be overlooked and ignored. Jesus confronted situations he found enraging because of their ungodly or demonic nature. When the unhealthy structures of religion replace the healthy responses of faith, anger is appropriate for persons of faith.

When Do You Stop Turning the Other Cheek?

Some Christians have been taught to turn the other cheek in the face of offense. We've been led in some cases to believe that Christians don't even feel anger; we merely settle for "righteous indignation." However, the New Testament frankly depicts Jesus' anger. Note two incidents in Mark 3 and Matthew 21 when religion had become sick and how Jesus responded angrily to these episodes.

Mark 3 provides a stark example of the ire of Jesus. Mark 1 and 2 show how quickly Jesus' ministry had ignited the popular imagination and how Jesus was functioning independently from the Pharisees' rules about the Sabbath. In reaction, the opposition parties were already gunning for him (Mark 2:24). The confrontation in Mark 3 demonstrates how, amid conflict, feelings often become the "facts" of the case. The actual facts were clear. There were (1) a handicapped person, (2) a Sabbath worship setting, and (3) the power to heal. But the negative feelings of the opposition became the overriding reality; bias was raised above compassion, an occurrence not uncommon when conflict boils.

In this case, the "feel equals real" equation is obvious. "Reality" became what was felt. Jesus noted how the opposition valued power, rules, and tradition more than health, wholeness, and compassion. They asked, "Is it lawful?" Instead, Jesus asked, "Is it merciful?" Their misplaced priority riled Jesus. Two paraphrases of verse 5 state the issue graphically. "Looking around at them angrily, for He was deeply disturbed by their indifference to human need . . ." (Mark 3:5, *LB*). Or, "He looked around at them in anger and, deeply distressed at their stubborn hearts . . ." (Mark 3:5, *NIV*). The Greek expression used for anger in this verse describes a snort of physical reaction. Jesus was obviously angry that the Pharisees had deliberately closed their hearts. There's no other way to interpret this incident. It's important to remember that only a lively conscience reacts spontaneously to wrong with appropriate anger.

Jesus healed the man's withered hand before the worshipping group. Immediately, also in rage, the Pharisees began cultivating an alliance with the Herodians and made their plans to gang up on Jesus. These groups could have announced, "We feel what we feel, therefore, it's real." Or "My mind's made up. Don't confuse me with facts" could have been the motto of these opposition groups. When institutionalized religion becomes diseased, responsible leaders get angry and act to change things.

Matthew 21 records another act of defiance and another instance of Jesus' anger. Here again perverted religion is reason enough for conflict. Once in a while folks elect themselves gatekeepers and decide who fits in and who doesn't. They create barriers by policies or attitudes to shut the "outs" out and bring the "ins" in. Those discriminating policies and attitudes may range from the sublime to the ridiculous.

In Matthew 21, Jesus encountered a group of religious gate-keepers and cleaned them out of the Temple. The money changers and dove sellers had created complicated rules and expensive price mark-ups for obtaining sacrifices. As a result, some of the faithful couldn't afford the fees equaling a half-day's wage for sacrificial animals. Others had become so discouraged by the hassle that they had finally given up entirely on worship in the Temple. When Jesus saw common persons were excluded from drawing close to God, he exploded and made the sparks fly. He flushed the offenders out of the Temple courts. Then he healed the blind and lame. Artificial barriers to worship angered Jesus. Again, the reaction of the gatekeepers was to look for a way to destroy Jesus (Mark 11:18).

Remember that this same Jesus counseled his followers to turn the other cheek on occasion (Matthew 5:39). These seemingly contradictory pieces of advice raise a tough question for us. When do you "turn over tables" rather than "turn cheeks?" That's a pivotal question when the stewardship of anger is at stake.

Turning Points

Answering the ongoing question of turning tables or turning cheeks involves several responses. Each of these responses is a kind of turning point, a reminder perhaps that the Old and New Testament writers called repentance a fundamental "turning" when lives and purposes changed directions. At least three occasions for turning are flagged for us in these two episodes of conflict.

__Turn over tables when your core values are endangered.__ Staying flexible on fringe issues while never compromising core values was the primary principle Jesus used. Leaders are always pushed to determine the principles they will apply to conflict situations. Master mediators Fisher and Ury in Getting to Yes[1] *have proposed four guidelines for conflict resolution efforts.*

—*People: Separate the people from the problem.*
—*Interests: Focus on interests, not positions.*
—*Options: Generate a variety of possibilities before deciding what to do.*
—*Criteria: Insist that the result be based on some objective standard.*

Conflict forces us to distinguish between the central and the peripheral. What conflict doesn't do automatically is turn us toward the center. The strategy of identifying and applying a foundational principle or principles in the face of conflicting issues is as old as the Garden of Eden. Principles draw non-negotiable "lines in the sand" as well as raise awareness of peripheral matters. Gardens have perimeters and centers, typically. The Garden of Eden was no exception. Note the flow of the story.

Now the Lord God had planted a garden in the east, in Eden; and there he put the man he had formed. And the Lord God made all kinds of trees grow out of the ground—trees that were pleasing to the eye and good for food. In the middle of the garden were the tree of life and the tree of the knowledge of good and evil (Genesis 2:8-9).

The Lord God took the man and put him in the Garden of Eden to work it and take care of it. And the Lord God commanded the man, 'You are free to eat from any tree in the garden; but you must not eat from the tree of the knowledge of good and evil, for when you eat of it you will surely die' (Genesis 2:15-17).

The woman said to the serpent, 'We may eat fruit from the trees in the garden, but God did say, "You must not eat fruit from the tree that is in the middle of the garden, and you must not touch it or you will die"' (Genesis 3:2-3).

Everything around the edges of the garden was available to Adam

*and Eve. The center, however, was off-limits to them. And, there
lies the temptation, doesn't it?*

Turn over tables when idols replace faithful living. *Conflict
smokes out our idols at the core or the "hot spot" of our lives. But
conflict doesn't automatically turn us from them. God has a way
of confronting our arenas of vulnerability and demanding access
to them. In Mark 3, the Pharisees held the power of interpreting
the rules. Even when obvious need was at stake they refused to be
concerned for anything but their power. In Matthew 21, the object
of the money makers was profit. Again, they had no interest in
yielding that concern. In both situations, confrontation was necessary to nudge the stalemate off dead center.*

C.S. Lewis in Mere Christianity[2] *applies a potent image of
remodeling a house to describe the confrontation of religious
conversion. Such a radical turning identifies our idols:*

> *God comes to rebuild that house. At first, perhaps, you can
> understand what He is doing. He is getting the drains right
> and stopping the leaks in the roof and so on: you knew that
> those jobs needed doing and so you were not surprised. But
> presently he starts knocking the house about in a way that
> hurts abominably and does not seem to make sense. What on
> earth is He up to? The explanation is that He is building quite
> a different house from the one you thought of—throwing up a
> new wing here, putting on an extra floor there, running up
> towers, making courtyards. You thought you were going to be
> made into a decent little cottage: but He is building a palace.
> He intends to come and live in it Himself.*

German theologian Helmut Thielicke in How the World
Began[3] *observes a similar pattern in human nature and in the
nature of God:*

> *God never comes through the door
> that I hold open for him,
> but always knocks*

at the one place
which I have walled up with concrete,
because I want it for myself alone.
But if I do not let him in there,
he turns away altogether.

Maybe that's why Jesus confronted perverted religion as he did.
Could it be that he knew we aren't likely to turn away from our
idols until we are confronted directly? Could it be that he saw
these confrontations as last chances to turn lives God-ward before
God turned away from them?

Turn over tables when "religion" tries to pervert faith. Jesus
confronted the structures of religion in these cases because the
attitudes, policies, and rules were attempting to squelch the spirit,
fire, and purpose of living faith. Sick religion cannot be allowed to
prosper unnoticed or unchallenged. Unfortunately, institutions
can tame the faithful and cow them.

A general observation about conflict may be timely here.
Conflict allows us to observe our psychological reactions to threat.
Do you turn toward the fray or turn tail and run from threats?
Shortly after the turn of this century, the psychologist W. B. Can-
non described the "fight-flight" syndrome. He claimed that our
reactions to threat and conflict were primitive responses. For
example, when the caveman found himself face-to-face with a
saber-toothed tiger in some prehistoric jungle clearing, the cave-
man had only two options. He could either fight for his life or run
for his life. Either way, his odds of surviving were essentially, as
Dizzy Dean used to say, "slim and none."

More recently, psychologists have noted that the fight-flight
response has physical components. Where do your energy and
adrenaline flow when you perceive a threat? Popular lore de-
scribes this near-electric surge of energy graphically. Does your
energy flow upward and give you the "hot head" of a fighter? Or,
does your energy flow downward and give you the "cold feet" of
one who flees?

Perhaps one way to look at the seemingly contradictory statements of Jesus about table turning and cheek turning is to consider the direction of energy flow. We can choose to use our angry hot-headedness for change when issues are crucial. We can choose to turn our cheeks, refuse to retaliate, and walk away when issues are trivial and the outcomes don't matter much.

In summary, under the pressure of conflict, it becomes doubly important that leaders know what to overturn and what to turn away from. It's certain that Jesus considered some things significant enough to dig in his heels and confront directly. He was incensed when human need was ignored in favor of worship rules. Jesus asserted, "The sabbath was made for humankind, not humankind for the sabbath" (Mark 2:27, NRSV). Furthermore, he detested religion perverted for personal gain. Jesus quoted the prophets with devastating force, "Is it not written: 'My house will be called a house of prayer for all nations'? But you have made it 'a den of robbers'" (Mark 11:17, NIV). These issues were important enough to violate Jesus' principles and to make him hotheaded.

Only Discriminating Persons Need to Apply

Wanted: Leaders who know the important from the unimportant and act accordingly.

Wanted: Leaders who can sort feelings from facts and use both.

Wanted: Leaders who function by principle amid conflict.

Wanted: Leaders who are alert to their private idols and personal demons.

Wanted: Leaders who know how they react to threat and conflict—and who guard against losing their leadership through a pattern of inappropriate responses.

* * * * *

CHAPTER XV

What to Do When There Are Two Sides and You're in the Middle

(Peacemaking/Paul in 1 Corinthians)

Conflict happens in all kinds of organizations. Sometimes, unfortunately, leaders find themselves in that no man's land called the middle when both extremes are displeased with any action you attempt.

Some Parties Aren't Fun or Funny

Corinth was Paul's problem church. In a way, it should be no surprise that the Corinthian church was troubled. Corinth was a wide open town—low morals, pagan religions, and easy money. In the ancient world, "to corinthianize" was shorthand for "to sin." That's not exactly the most favorable setting for a new congregation.

Survey the internal landscape of the congregation in Corinth for land mines. Look at the list of issues: Lawsuits (1 Corinthians 6:1-11), sexual impurity (1 Corinthians 5), abuse of spiritual gifts (1 Corinthians 12-14), and factions (1 Corinthians 3). Tthe Corinthian church was a cauldron of simmering conflicts. Any of these problems taken by itself—money, sex, religion, or power—is a potent conflict possibility by itself. Stir the whole mix together, and the buried land mines become a collection of grenades with the pins pulled.

Parties were the order of the day within the Corinthian church. These parties weren't occasions for relaxation and enjoyment, however. Rather, they were cliques or factions and weren't fun or funny. Factionalism's power issue is almost always divisive. Corinth had its power plays between the Paul Party, the Apollos Party, the Cephas Party, and the Christ Party (1 Corinthians 1:10-17). As Paul described it,

> . . . there are quarrels among you . . . One of you says, 'I follow Paul'; another 'I follow Apollos'; another 'I follow Cephas'; still another 'I follow Christ' (1 Corinthians 1:13, *NIV*).

Each group apparently recruited followers and built allegiances. Paul was caught in the middle, the likely object for being drawn into alliances and/or being attacked by various interest groups. Either or both.

Paul took three decisive actions to confront these factions. First, he appealed to them in Christ's name to cooperate with each other (1 Corinthians 1:10). Paul saw Christ as the basic unifier amid diversity. Second, he defined himself and announced that he was a minister and missionary, not a politician or party leader (1 Corinthians 1:13-17). Paul said "No thanks" to leading any faction. Third, Paul pointed out that only Christ has died for the church (1 Corinthians 1:18-31). The message is clear: only Christ owns the church. No matter how much believers may love or serve or sacrifice for their congregation, not one of them atoned for that local church. The church belongs to Christ alone.

Suggestions for the Leader in the Middle

Leaders in conflict situations need all the help they can get—congregationally, attitudinally, theologically, and strategically. Paul's experience in Corinth offers help in exactly those areas.

Congregationally, differences enrich us. A casual reading of Paul's listings of spiritual gifts in 1 Corinthians 12 and 14 pushes us toward an obvious conclusion: diversity doesn't need to wedge us apart. Why? Because we're all parts of Christ's body (1 Corinthians 12:27). Because we have the same God working within us (1 Corinthians 12:6). Because our gifts are for the common good (1 Corinthians 12:7). Because every gift has its own unique and vital function (1 Corinthians 12:14-26). Although Paul notes roughly thirty spiritual gifts in the "for instance" listings contained in his writings, the inescapable conclusion is that our various gifts can—and must—enrich, build up, and complement the corporate life of congregations. Differences can enrich rather than divide us.

Attitudinally, forgiveness opens the door for conflict management. For leaders caught in the midst of conflict, the Corinthian correspondence contains some helpful guidelines. For one thing, Paul uses an accounting term to note that the Christ kind of love keeps no ledger sheet of wrongs (1 Corinthians 13:5). Peacemakers don't fret with creating a paper trail or record of grievances for future reference. Forgiving someone offers a first step for dealing with factional conflict. Forgiveness paves the way for God to do his work of reconciliation in persons and organizations.

Theologically, peacemaking and reconciliation are two different activities and have two distinct initiators. Reconciliation is one of Paul's special themes. Paul's emphasis on peacemaking and reconciliation is consistent throughout his writings. Leaders may assist with peacemaking and conflict management, but only Christ can reconcile and make friends of enemies. Leaders are called on to become peacemaking agents in preparation for God's reconciliation.

> *. . . if anyone is in Christ, he is a new creation; the old has gone, the new has come! All this is from God, who reconciled us to himself through Christ and gave us the ministry of*

*reconciliation: that God was reconciling the world to himself
in Christ, not counting men's sins against them. And he has
committed to the message of reconciliation (2 Corinthians
5:17-19).*

*Leaders are called on to function as peacemakers, dealing with
differences comes naturally with the territory of leadership.
Peacemaking has its limits, however. When we see full-fledged
enemies become new-found friends, God has been at work in His
world.*

*Strategically, leaders can avoid factionalizing alliances . . .
If we stay clear about our visions and values. If we sort out our
idols from our principles. If we remain alert to opposing and
seducing forces around us. If we are willing to say "oops," apolo-
gize, and back out when we accidentally wander into an alliance.
These approaches permitted Paul to avoid the entanglements of
conflict.*

*Triangles are the most common shape of social conflict. That
is, most arguments boil down to two folks in stalemate with each
other who are both trying desperately to draw another person (or
issue) into the disagreement in order to break the tie. Instinctively,
we all know that two against one creates pretty good odds. So, we
look for an ally with whom we can triangle so we can set up an
"odd man out" situation against our opponent.*

*Applying family systems theories, Ed Friedman has identified
seven laws of emotional triangles common to social systems.[1]
These guides help us understand why peacemaking becomes such a
difficult leadership challenge in congregations and "counsel" us
to stay out of triangles.*

*1. Unhealthy relationships are generally kept in balance by a
third party.*

*2. Third parties in triangles are rarely able to change the
relationship between the other two triangled persons.*

3. Attempts to change other triangled persons tend to backfire and may cost us our relationships with the other persons in the triangle.

4. The third party in triangled change efforts usually ends up with the stress (and blame) of the relational triangle.

5. Trying to change one triangle within a larger social system ordinarily draws resistance from across the broader system, owing to systems' basic preference for stability over change.

6. Unhealthy systems focus conflict primarily on one side of the triangle, making that focal relationship more vulnerable to conflict as well as less flexible and creative.

7. We can bring change only to those relationships in which we have a direct relationship. That is, change is made possible by self-defining within relationships and allowing others to react to that initiative.

Unfortunately, in the heat of battle, any alliance—no matter how destructive or unholy it may become in the long run—seems helpful and righteous enough as long as we're seeing red. But, triangles are rarely helpful or healthful. In social systems, like congregations and families, if any part of the corporate body loses, is wounded, or gets lopped off, the entire body is diminished. Paul makes this point forcefully, "If one part suffers, every part suffers with it . . ." (1 Corinthians 12:26, NIV). The health of the overall body depends on the well-being of every part of the body.

Part of the Solution, Not Part of the Problem

Wanted: Leaders who aren't naive about power's potential and who are willing to use that potential for good rather than evil.

Wanted: Leaders who know that disruptions can open the door for constructive change.

Wanted: Leaders who can refuse the seductive efforts of factions in favor of the well-being of the entire group.

Wanted: Leaders who don't carry grudges.

Wanted: Leaders who are ready to take the risks of peacemaking.

Wanted: Leaders who appreciate differences.

Wanted: Leaders who can stay out of triangles.

* * * * *

CHAPTER XVI

So the Boss Is Crazy!

(David and Saul in 1 Samuel 16-31)

Many of us have been supervised by difficult bosses at one time or another. Fortunately, few of us have had bosses who tried to murder us. That's where David has something to teach us.

The Twilight Zone of Success

Saul wasn't always crazy. In fact, the first king of Israel was initially a commanding figure, a courageous and charismatic warrior, and a leader with a sensitive conscience. Chosen king as a result of the popular clamor for a fit successor to Samuel, Saul led effective military campaigns, probably breaking the Philistines' monopoly on iron products (1 Samuel 13 and 14) and turning back the Amalekite threat (1 Samuel 15). During these early successes in his reign, Saul kept the religious and political functions separate by calling Israel to battle using both his name and seer Samuel's in the rallying cry (1 Samuel 11:7). Saul's impatience, however, soon caused him to overstep his bounds and fill a religious as well as a political role, resulting ultimately in his rejection as king by Samuel (1 Samuel 13:14).

Once rejected as king, Saul became increasingly moody and emotionally unbalanced. Abandoned by Samuel (1 Samuel 15:35)

and overshadowed by David's popularity and success (1 Samuel
18:7-9), Saul displayed a psychological oscillation between white
hot frenzies of energy and black pits of depression. For example,
when Saul was made king, in rapid-fire and manic fashion he fell
into ecstatic prophesying, rescued the city of Jabesh, and led
military strikes against the Philistines and Amalekites (1 Samuel
10-15). In contrast, Saul also became increasingly susceptible to
blue, depressed states of torment. During these times of depression, only David the court minstrel could soothe Saul with his
music (1 Samuel 16:14-23).

After joining Saul's court, David rose through the ranks
quickly. He became Saul's armor-bearer (1 Samuel 16:21), victor
over Goliath (1 Samuel 17), and a man to be watched—literally.

> Whatever Saul sent him to do, David did it so successfully that
> Saul gave him a high rank in the army. This pleased all the
> people, and Saul's officers as well.
> When the men were returning home after David had killed the
> Philistine, the women came out from all the towns of Israel to
> meet King Saul with singing and dancing, with joyful songs
> and with tambourines and lutes. As they danced, they sang:
> "Saul has slain his thousands,
> and David his tens of thousands."
> Saul was very angry; this refrain galled him. "They have
> credited David with tens of thousands," he thought, "but me
> with only thousands. What more can he get but the king-
> dom?" And from that time on Saul kept a jealous eye on
> David (1 Samuel 18:5-9, *NIV*).

Calling what Saul did to David merely keeping "a jealous eye"
on him is a master stroke of understatement. Look at what turning
green with envy caused Saul to do to David. Twice in melancholy
and rage Saul attempted to spear David (1 Samuel 18:9-16 and
19:9-10). Additionally, Saul tried to turn marriage into a snare for
David (1 Samuel 18:21), to influence Jonathan and his servants to

kill David (1 Samuel 19:1), to dispatch his police to capture David while he slept (1 Samuel 19:11-17), and to conduct far-flung searches for the fleeing David. In the process, Saul butchered the priests of Nob who had unwittingly helped David and his band (1 Samuel 22:11-20). That's more than a jealous eye. That's a crazy boss!

In reaction, David twice refused to kill Saul and even forbade his men to strike out against the person David saw as under God's protection (1 Samuel 24 and 26). In order to get some distance from Saul, David and his 600 bandits hired out to the Philistine leader, Achish, as raiders. David thought: "The best thing I can do is to escape to the land of the Philistines. Then Saul will give up searching for me anywhere in Israel, and I will slip out of his hand" (1 Samuel 27:1, *NIV*).

For sixteen months, David stayed out of Saul's way in the town of Ziklag. In the meantime, Saul's mood worsened. In desperation, he took counsel with the witch of Endor (1 Samuel 28) and, facing defeat by the Philistines, finally committed suicide (1 Samuel 31:4). Then David was anointed the second king (2 Samuel 2:1-7) and became the boss himself.

Coping with Bad Bosses

Grothe and Wylie in Problem Bosses[1] *identify a rogue's gallery of bad bosses. According to them, some bosses are living proof of* The Peter Principle[2] *and have risen to their levels of incompetence. Others are too nice, too excitable, too tyrannical, too bureaucratic and "by the book," addicted, sexual exploiters, away too much, pathological liars, or too egotistical. How would you like to work for a boss whose definition of leadership is "the ability to inflict pain?"[3] That could be a "problem," couldn't it?*

A research project at the Center for Creative Leadership has identified one specific type of boss who's tough on supervisees as well as on herself or himself: the expansive boss.[4] Expansive personalities reach for mastery and intend to achieve big goals in big ways. Goal-oriented and task-centered leaders would say, "That's good! Right?" Not necessarily. Any ability, when over-used, can become a liability.

Expansiveness, when overdone, can also become a weakness. How? Some heavily task-focused bosses get the job done—at the expense of their workers and to the detriment of group morale. They take personal offense at inadequate performance while taking good work for granted. They rail out against marginal production but rarely show positive support for strong performers. Expansive bosses may adopt an arrogant air of royalty and trade in a strong sense of self for an overblown ego and the quest for self-expansion and elevation. They pursue control rather than empowering others. When such a pattern becomes predominate in bosses' behaviors, they are well on their way to winning lots of battles but losing the war.

What options are open to a follower whose leader is techni-cally incompetent, emotionally unbalanced, or relationally insensi-tive? The David and Saul saga suggests some beginning points for coping with bad bosses.

David was forced to deal with a difficult boss. His actions provide some possibilities for us in the face of poor supervision. Note what David did.

(1) He stayed out of the line of fire. David had to dodge actual spears and must have learned to stay alert, protect himself, and take no unnecessary personal risks.

(2) He listened to and heeded the grapevine. David's friend-ship with Saul's son Jonathan gave him inside information from Saul's inner sanctum—information that David used literally to save his life (1 Samuel 20).

(3) He accepted others' protection on occasion. Both Jonathan and Michael interceded for David (1 Samuel 19 and 20) and spared him some jeopardy.

(4) He refused to attack the boss. David steadfastly resisted

the temptation to speak ill of or retaliate against Saul. *Revenge was recommended by others, but never entertained as a legitimate option for David himself.*

(5) *He functioned consistently amid his responsibilities. Never had David acted in anything but Saul's best interests. For in-stance, after both opportunities to kill Saul, David asserted his basic allegiance to the king:* "I am not guilty of wrongdoing or rebellion" *(1 Samuel 24:11). Again, he asked,* "What have I done, and what wrong am I guilty of?" *(1 Samuel 26:18).*

(6) *He found another job. Although David was driven into banditry by Saul's craziness, he chose to move away from Saul rather than endanger himself further and enrage the king.*

Cultivating Sane Supervisors and Bosses Who Bless

Wanted: Leaders who are emotionally constant and relationally steady.

Wanted: Leaders who can help their followers succeed and not feel threatened by others' success.

Wanted: Leaders who guard against turning an over-used strength into an unproductive weakness.

Wanted: Leaders who have strong egos rather than big egos.

Wanted: Leaders who bless and empower their followers instead of inflicting pain.

* * * * *

CHAPTER XVII

Big Wins, Big Losses

(Failure/Elijah in 1 Kings 18-19)

Success isn't all wins. Some losses are inevitable—even for the most successful leaders. Elijah learned that leaders are especially vulnerable after a big win.

High Noon on Mount Carmel

There was a shootout at the OK Corral in the Old Testament. When Elijah faced the priests of Baal on Mount Carmel, a religious line was drawn in the sand and a spiritual duel arranged. The stakes were high, and the sides were obvious. At high noon one solitary hero in a white hat stood silhouetted in Main Street against hundreds of bad guys in black hats.

The stories about Elijah actually cover very few pages in the Bible, but his influence is profound and widespread throughout the Scriptures. Elijah burst on the biblical scene as both a messenger and an activist. Consequently, Elijah was seen by the king as "troubler of Israel" (1 Kings 18:16), a person with a troublesome message and a meddlesome attitude.

Ahab ruled as king of the Northern Kingdom about nine centuries before Christ when Elijah stepped forward to challenge the system by word and deed. Ahab was a bad guy par excellence.

He viewed the sins of his predecessors as trivial. He therefore entered into a political marriage with the foreigner Jezebel, a woman whose name has become synonymous with evil and shamelessness. Jezebel worshipped Baal, an offense that seemed to call for Elijah's brand of frontier justice. The bottom line evaluation of Ahab was devastating:

> Ahab . . . did more to provoke the Lord, the God of Israel, to anger than did all the kings of Israel before him (1 Kings 16:33, *NIV*).

Elijah confronted Ahab, summoned the nation to gather on Mount Carmel, and called out 850 of the rival priests. Elijah accused the nation of wavering between two deities: God and Baal. They stood silent. So Elijah proposed a simple test to determine who was the true object of worship. A sacrifice would be prepared and the deity who sent fire would be proven the real god. The people liked that kind of demonstration.

The Baal priests called on their god, but, after a futile morning of pleading, no fire fell. At high noon, Elijah began taunting them with questions about their god. Was he distracted or busy or vacationing? The frantic Baalites redoubled their efforts, even slashing themselves until they bled. Still, during the afternoon no fire fell.

When evening arrived, Elijah's turn had come. He rebuilt the altar, using twelve stones to represent Israel's tribes. He ordered water to saturate the sacrifice. Then he called on God to reveal his power, and the fire fell. The people fell, too. They fell on their faces and declared God as their Lord. Finally, the people arose and killed the priests of Baal. That OK Corral on top of Mount Carmel was littered with the bodies of the bad guys.

Elijah had prevailed in a dramatic, public confrontation. He had won. He had gone from rags to riches. But his success was about to sour. He was going to make a quick journey from riches back to rags.

Ahab sent a succinct notice to Elijah: You'll be dead within twenty-four hours (1 Kings 19:2). The same prophet who boldly had faced the king, 850 rivals, and a wishy-washy nation earlier in the day now panicked and ran for his life. By the next day Elijah was so completely dispirited he asked God to take his life. Isn't it ironic that so radical a turnaround happened so rapidly to the great prophet? Elijah had plummeted from elation to depression and desperation in one day's time. He had tasted both the nectar of victory and the gall of defeat, almost in the same swallow.

The "Elijah Trap" of depression after achieving a major goal can occur for several reasons when leaders face loss.

> I have been very zealous for the Lord God Almighty. The Israelites have rejected your covenant, broken down your altars, and put your prophets to death with the sword. I am the only one left, and now they are trying to kill me too (1 Kings 19:10, *NIV*).

(1) Elijah developed the tunnel vision so common in zealots. He had contended singlemindedly for right and now might lose everything. (2) He saw himself as indispensable, as God's last and only hope. (3) He felt isolated. (4) He feared for his life. Taken together, these concerns can easily trigger discouragement.

God shook Elijah out of his despondency. He prescribed rest, food, exercise, privacy, and face-to-face communication. When Elijah traveled to Horeb, God's mountain, he still thought he was the only faithful prophet God had left. But God sent Elijah back into the fray with two encouraging words: (1) there are seven thousand other faithful so you aren't alone, and (2) the next generation of leaders is prepared and selected, so go anoint Jehu and Elisha (1 Kings 19:14-18).

Can't Win Them All

Successful leaders soon learn that no one wins all the time. They agree with singer Beverly Sills: "You may be disappointed if you fail, but you are doomed if you don't try." Good leaders learn, with Elijah, that leadership development begins with self-development; they see leadership as the stewardship of their best self. So the Elijah's of the world put lots of effort into self-examination.

First, successful leaders are typically self-aware. Perhaps Elijah had spent so much time in desert solitude that he didn't know himself well enough in social settings. Good leaders know themselves in all situations. (1) Effective leaders stay on an even keel. They admit that "you can't win' em all," even though they may try. Good leaders intend to win, but can shake off inevitable losses. In the face of loss, they adopt the French motto, "Ce n'est pas la fin du monde," or, "It's not the end of the world." They look toward another day. (2) They recognize the expenditure of mental, physical, and spiritual energy that excellence demands. Lord Nelson, for example, England's naval hero, never overcame his tendency toward seasickness. He confronted his personal weakness, paid the price for excellence in discipline, and finally destroyed Napoleon's fleet. (3) Good leaders face reality. They know the risks of 1:850 odds, but they learn to count the advantages of a 7000:1 majority too. (4) The best leaders fail frequently—because they take the risks of trying new approaches and therefore of making mistakes. Only mediocre leaders play so safely that they make no mistakes.

Second, successful leaders are adept at self-care. Adequate rest and recreation as well as a balanced diet are basic self-care strategies, as Elijah discovered. Some therapists are now using physical exercise as a primary treatment for psychological depression; they may even drop off counselees in an isolated setting and force them to walk home as a method of breaking the cycle of despondency! Healthy self-care reminds us that body and soul are closely related.

*Third, successful leaders **control their self-talk**. All of us have internal conversations with ourselves. Sometimes our self-talk takes the form of positive "pep talks." Remember the children's story about* The Little Engine That Could? *That little engine's self-talk centered on optimistic, "I think I can" attitudes. Depressed persons, however, literally talk themselves out of succeeding by negative, doubt-full "pity talks." They learn helplessness and talk themselves into defeat with "I can't do anything right" and "Bad things always happen to me" and "I mess up every time." Motivation expert Martin Seligman in* Learned Optimism *teaches us how to achieve an optimistic outlook on life, a necessary ingredient for success. Interestingly, studies indicate that religion provides hope to overcome depression.[1] Elijah could have been a subject for these studies! His self-talk was dripping with doubt and pessimism, but it changed when he responded to the "gentle whisper" (1 Kings 19:12).*

Wanted:
Champions Who Can Make Comebacks

Wanted: Leaders who have the courage to risk.

Wanted: Leaders who are willing to stand alone, if necessary.

Wanted: Leaders who practice self-care and are good stewards of themselves.

Wanted: Leaders who can master their self-talk and turn their internal conversations toward optimistic goals.

Wanted: Leaders who major in self-awareness, minimize their blindspots, and overcome their weaknesses.

Wanted: Leaders who appreciate successes and rebound after failures, who can make the "rags to riches" climb.

* * * * *

Influence:
Can Great Leadership Happen
from Behind the Scenes?

There is no leadership without power and influence. Leaders use whatever leverage they have to attempt to achieve goals. Influence is a bottom line intention of effective leaders.

Influence has to do with producing an effect by means, either direct or indirect, that have an impact or consequence. Someone or something becomes empowered when the stewardship of influence is used well. Power, of course, comes in several currencies, through teamwork, by anticipating the future, and by example, to name the ones dealt with in the three chapters of this section.

Too often it's assumed that only charismatic individuals are leaders. The classic Great Man theory of leadership, while true at times, is probably too individualistic and heroic for real life. This section raises up several lesser-known groups in the Bible for our instruction in the arts of leadership. These groups call several issues to our attention.

  −Leaders act as teambuilders.
  −Leaders act with planned intentionality.
  −Leaders act as models and mentors for others.

Recurring themes in the three chapters of this section point to some ways leaders multiply their influence:

(1) Leaders increase their impact by developing effective teams.

Leaders realize that a group can achieve things that an individual can't—and they act to build teams.

(2) Leaders plan intentionally to meet their pacesetting opportunities. We frequently don't see clearly where God is acting, but by preparing for leadership and by planning as well as we can, leaders are ready with ideas when doors of opportunity open.

(3) Leaders model themselves after the positive features of others' leadership approaches. Leaders observe other leaders, read biographies, become "people detectives" in order to understand what makes others effective, and invite quality mentorship from able leaders.

CHAPTER XVIII

The Twelve —
Team or Trouble?

(Teambuilding/The Twelve in Mark 3:13-19)

The Twelve were some crew! Look at the roster. A turncoat. A pair of blood brothers. A political radical. A doubter. A traitor. And several faces in the crowd. Would you place the leadership responsibility for the future of world redemption in those twenty-four distinctly diverse hands? What an unlikely, risky, troublesome gang! Or, what faith and teambuilding!

The Twelve: Team-in-Training or Trouble-in-Waiting?

Jesus chose and commissioned twelve very different persons. This assortment of unique persons was offered three crucial leadership opportunities. (1) The Twelve were to "be with him" (Mark 3:14, *NIV*). Relationally, they had the opportunity to watch him minister and lead firsthand. Jesus knew his vision and style were more apt to be caught than taught. Additionally, they were to become a support group for him and for each other. (2) He would "send them out to preach" (Mark 3:14, *NIV*). Redemptively, they would invite persons into God's kingdom. (3) They would "have authority to drive out demons" (Mark 3:15, *NIV*). The restorative task of giving persons health and wholeness was also a wonderful opportunity afforded to those whom he designated. Relate, redeem, and restore—that's what they did.

As in all group settings, the Twelve were leaders at some points and followers at others. While learning to become apostles, their productive work was understandably uneven and fairly unpredictable. Therefore, their attempts at leadership and followership varied considerably in effectiveness from situation to situation. A quick survey of the Twelve as leader-followers depicts their differences.[1]

Simon Peter, named first in all four lists of the Twelve (Mark 3:16-19, Matthew 10:2-4, Luke 6:14-16, and Acts 1:13-26), was typically first to speak and act—usually with vigor but sometimes with inconsistency. On the one hand, Peter showed his faith, especially in the Pentecost sermon in Acts 2. He was, on the other hand, slow to share the Gospel with the Gentiles (Acts 10). Peter often needed direction, but when shown, he took risks willingly (John 13:9, John 21:15-19, and John 1:41-42).

Andrew didn't display the personal charisma of his brother, Simon Peter, but he did show more consistency in his leadership and followership. His constant missionary spirit was evident in bringing Simon (John 1:41-42), the boy whose lunch fed the 5,000 (John 6:8-9), and the Greeks (John 12:20-26) to Jesus. Andrew treated every challenge as another opportunity to introduce someone else to Jesus.

Aggressive brothers James and John were quick to exercise initiative, although their zeal wasn't always positive. Harshly, they counseled a firestorm for a Samaritan village (Luke 9:51-56). Narrowly, they asked for the most powerful positions in the messianic kingdom (Mark 10:35-45). Later, they apparently mellowed and became influential pacesetters in the early church.

Philip was a cautious visionary who knew what to do, but was slow to act on his knowledge. In John 12, the visiting Greeks asked the Greek-named Philip about Jesus. Taking a low-risk stance, he instead allowed Andrew to bring the Leader and the visitors together.

The record is sketchy for the rest of the Twelve. Thomas has become famous—or infamous—for his questioning approach to life. Judas has become infamous—and famous—for betraying Jesus. The remaining half of the Twelve, including replacement Matthias, have left few clues about their approaches to leadership or followership.

At the conclusion of His ministry, Jesus prayed for the Twelve and all others who believed in Him.

> My prayer is . . . that all of them may be one . . . . May they be brought to complete unity to let the world know that you sent me . . . (John 17:20-23, *NIV*).

Jesus worked to mold a unified team from a gang of individuals. He knew that "team" has no "I" in it. Jesus also recognized that the Twelve and others would have to carry on the work of the Kingdom after He was gone and no longer led the team directly.

Diversity Enriches Teams—and Leaders

Effective leaders recognize that diversity enriches teams because leadership is always a shared responsibility. At any point in time, followers can step forward to accept responsibility and spell the leader. The natural world seems to understand automatically the advantages of shared leadership. Take the V formations of migrating geese as an example. Engineers have used wind tunnel tests to calibrate why geese always use the V formation. Here's what they discovered. Each goose by flapping its wings creates lift for the goose flying next in formation. The entire flock gains 71% greater flying range in formation over solo flight. Periodically the lead goose in the V formation falls back and lets another leader move forward to take the point. During long migratory flights, every goose at one time or other takes the point and leads. Each goose is different, and each contributes to the flock's effectiveness. Teamwork between leaders and followers makes the most of pacesetting opportunities.

Max DePree, furniture manufacturing CEO, in Leadership Is
an Art *claims that respect for the differences in groups is a basic
perspective for good leadership:*

> *This begins with an understanding of the diversity of gifts.
> Understanding the diversity of these gifts enables us to begin
> taking the crucial step of trusting each other. It also enables
> us to begin to think in a new way about the strengths of others.
> Everyone comes with certain gifts—but not the same gifts.
> True participation and enlightened leadership allow these
> gifts to be expressed in different ways and at different times.[2]*

*Applying diverse abilities in different ways at different times calls
for teambuilding.*

*Why was teambuilding needed for the Twelve—or any other
work group? Check the following reasons to see which of them
apply to your own leadership opportunities. (1) Groups with
common tasks function best as teams rather than collections of
freelancers. (2) The natural diversity in most groups needs har-
nessing. (3) Teamwork guards against tasks falling between the
cracks. (4) A team outlook makes it less likely that the range of
talents in a group might go unused. (5) Team pride prevents sub-
standard production. (6) Teams are most effective when they are
clear and unified about their goals. (7) Team spirit builds morale.
(8) Teamwork lessens the chance of the leader, or of key followers,
feeling that "I'm the only one who's pulling his weight in this
outfit."*

*Teams allow us to do together what we can't accomplish singly.
Effective leaders learn to develop teamwork and concentrate on
building team spirit.*

Teambuilding—a Key Leadership Skill

Wanted: Leaders who are willing to build teams from diverse followers.

Wanted: Leaders who select followers who aren't "like me."

Wanted: Leaders who don't spell "team" with an "I."

Wanted: Leaders who are ready to take the point or to share responsibility for the good of the group.

Wanted: Leaders who appreciate the different gifts of their team members and try to open doors for all gifts to be used well.

Wanted: Leaders who realize more can be achieved together than individually.

* * * * *

CHAPTER XIX

Intentional Leadership — A Woman's Touch

(Planning/Women Leaders in Proverbs 31, Matthew 1 and Romans 16)

Leadership requires intentionality, a plan of action. Although women have frequently been overlooked and invisible in the leadership picture, the Bible identifies some important contributions by women to God's plan of redemption.

When Second Fiddles Played the Lead

The Bible is basically a man's book, written by men for men in masculine terms to address a masculine culture. Jewish men in the first century pointedly thanked God that they had not been born Gentiles, slaves, or women. It's surprising, therefore, to find so many women in the Bible step from background followership into foreground leadership. Given the cultural situation, it was an extremely long step for many of these women of faith.

Even a partial survey of key women leaders in the Bible identifies a myriad of situations in which females contributed directly to God's plan of redemption. In the Old Testament, Sarah made a difference in Hebrew history and had the last laugh when she gave birth to an heir to God's covenant, gaining for herself a place in the Faithful's Hall of Fame in Hebrews 11 (Genesis 18:10-

14, 21:1-3, and Hebrews 11:11). Deborah, a judge and prophetess, by "leading Israel" (Judges 4:4, *NIV*) delivered her nation from the Canaanites. (She was assisted, after a fashion, by Jael, Heber's wife, who assassinated the Canaanite commander by indelicately driving a tent peg through his temple!) Huldah, prophetess during Josiah's reign, provided leadership by confirming the words of Scripture for the king (2 Kings 22). Queen Esther exercised leadership when she risked her life to save her fellow Jews from an extermination plot.

That favorite Mother's Day sermon text in Proverbs 31 shows a woman taking initiative in planning, leading, buying, selling, and working. She wins the confidence of her family and the respect of her community. I once worked in a denominational agency where pay levels were determined by the strength of the verbs in your job description. For example, people who "created," "directed," or "supervised" made higher salaries than persons who "assisted," "monitored," or "guided." Look at the strength of the verbs used to describe this woman leader in Proverbs 31. She "selects" and "works" and "buys" and "supplies" and "laughs" and "speaks" and "watches over." She could have earned top dollar in a certain denominational agency I know! No wonder the Proverbist sums up her phenomenal list of accomplishments with praise: "Many women do noble things, but you surpass them all" (Proverbs 31:29, *NIV*).

The trend of significant women leaders continues in the New Testament. Two New Testament chapters, however, provide special insight into the leadership contribution of women. Scan Matthew 1 and Romans 16.

Have you looked closely at Jesus' family tree in Matthew 1 lately? It's an interesting structure in general, but four branches are especially intriguing. Four women—Rahab, Ruth, Tamar, and Bathsheba—are listed among Jesus' forebears. Each has a checkered past, two of them are members of hated races, and yet each is considered worthy to be noted as a pivotal person in the Saviour's lineage. A prostitute, two adulteresses, and a foreigner—all females and all in Jesus' family tree! (There are some similarly "interesting" males in the listing too.) What's the significance of such an unusual line-up? Matthew obviously intends to show that in God's design for redemption there are no distinctions. The barriers between races, genders, and creeds are flattened in the subtle references to these four women. Even in such a traditionally male document as a Jewish genealogy, woman are prominently noted as central contributors to and leaders in God's plan of redemptive history.

Study also Paul's personal greetings to the believing community in Romans 16. One quarter of the leaders mentioned in this chapter are women. Phoebe (Romans 16:1), listed first in the passage and likely the deliverer of the letter to Rome, helped set the pace of ministry in the New Testament church. In fact, Paul calls her a "champion" who had cared for many (Romans 16:2). Priscilla, mentioned second in this listing along with her husband Aquila, had stepped forward as a leading missionary strategist, minister, and fellow craftsman with Paul in Corinth and Ephesus. In Ephesus, she helped update the religious perspective of the teachable Apollos (Acts 18). Priscilla and Aquila had risked their lives and established a house church in their own dwelling (Romans 16:3-5). (Note Paul's order of address here. In four of the six New Testament passages referring to this husband and wife team, she is mentioned first.) Additionally in this chapter, Mary, Tryphena, Tryphosa, and the mother of Rufus are given special recognition for their efforts in behalf of the Good News.

More than any other book, Acts shows the dramatic spread of the Gospel across cultures and regions. Women planners and leaders contributed to the extension of the church. For example, Dorcas (Acts 9:36-39) ministered to the poor in Joppa. Likewise, Lydia (Acts 16:13-15), a merchant, made her home a base camp for the missionary enterprise. In short, God's plan for world redemption was—and is—gender inclusive.

The Helping Hand Strikes Again!

Generally speaking, research indicates that women are better planners than men.[1] That may be why women leaders appear at strategic points in the Bible. Socialized differently than males, women are apparently superior to men in several qualities: responding to stress more slowly and selectively and, therefore, handling it better, dealing with unexpected and ambiguous events more comfortably, handling details more easily, involving and supporting followers more fully, negotiating in a manner that preserves longer-term relationships, and filling service-oriented work responsibilities better. These factors make women especially strong planners and strategists.

You've met women leaders like her. She's a human resources executive in a major real estate development company. She practices leadership intentionally. One of her strengths is getting people together to talk, listen, resolve their differences, combine forces, and make plans. In other words, she takes those tender mothering and nurturing skills she's learned at home to work with her. But she can be tough too. In fact, her co-workers tell her they can actually see her behavior switch from the naturally tender side to the less characteristic tough mode. They signal her changing roles to each other with this insightful phrase, "The helping hand . . . strikes again!"

Modern women leaders find it takes a combination of tenderness and toughness to break the "glass ceiling" that has traditionally kept women from ascending to the executive suite. But change is coming, at least at the middle management level. In the last twenty years, women middle managers have increased in number from twenty percent of the workforce to forty percent. Women have the same personality strengths as men, but their socialization process has sent them into the marketplace with a different set of skills. This different set of skills includes the knack for planning. Therefore, these unique abilities are beginning to be recognized as valuable talents at work.

Marilyn Loden in Feminine Leadership[2] *notes that our culture has encouraged women to show concern for people, develop interpersonal skills, and solve problems intuitively and creatively. Many women are stepping into career leadership using the same experience base they've developed as family and household managers. As a result, women have a strong service orientation, tend to be good orchestrators and mediators, and are able to build and preserve better support for group decisions. Whether helping hand or gloved fist, women are moving from followership to leadership in the business and religious worlds.*

Stepping from the Background
to the Foreground

Wanted: Leaders who know God transcends all cultures and stereotypes.

Wanted: Leaders who intentionally seize whatever leadership opportunities are presented to them.

Wanted: Leaders who fear neither tenderness nor toughness and who use both appropriately.

Wanted: Leaders who are able to get along with others—and who can mediate when conflict occurs.

Wanted: Leaders who care about persons, results, and consensus building.

* * * * *

CHAPTER XX

The "Be Like" Factor

(Modeling/Numbers 6, 1 Chronicles 25, Proverbs 1:1-7)

Models and mentors are important for leaders. Elijah mentored
Elisha. Paul served as a model for Silas. But, some important
leadership modeling occurred in the Bible by groups we usually
overlook.

Modeling the Way

It's tempting to turn the Bible into a book of heroic individual
leaders—Moses, David, Nehemiah, Ruth, Jesus, and Paul. They,
and other singular leaders, are obvious models and mentors for us.
However, there's much to be learned from some fairly obscure
leader groups hidden away in the pages of the biblical story. What
about the Nazarites, the directors of the temple choirs, and the
sages? What leadership insights can they demonstrate for today's
leaders? How can we "be like" them?

The Nazarites were holy men and women. These charismatic
figures took a "vow of separation" and kept themselves from wine
and grape products, from contact with corpses, and from haircuts
(Numbers 6:1-21). Well-known Nazarites included Samson and
Samuel. Some Nazarites were committed from birth to lifelong
vows, like the holy warrior Samson (Judges 13:7). Others volun-

tarily took time-limited vows for specific conduct. Perhaps the prophet Elisha's baldness was the result of completing a temporary Nazarite vow (2 Kings 2:23-25). The temporary pattern was probably the predominate approach by the time of the late monarchy.

The Nazarites modeled a calling and commitment to tradition. When the nomadic herdsmen of the Hebrews arrived in the Promised Land, they were challenged by the settled agricultural tribes to update their faith and adopt "city ways." Pressured to be modern and fit into their new culture, many of the Israelites abandoned the old ways. By the eighth century before Christ, Israel had, unfortunately, generally frustrated God's special calling of the Nazirites:

> I . . . raised up prophets from among your sons and Nazarites from among your young men . . . But you made the Nazirites drink wine and commanded the prophets not to prophesy (Amos 2:11-12, *NIV*).

Loyalty to the Deliverer God who brought Israel out of Egypt was, however, still valued by the Nazarites. Their commitment to holiness modeled a stricter, more traditional lifestyle.

The directors of the temple choirs were prophetic celebrants and (literally) tone-setters at regular and special worship occasions. These choristers shaped and helped lead the nation's worship. They collected psalms into hymnals and developed distinctive performance styles. The hymnbook of Asaph, for example, apparently included Psalm 50 as well as 73-83, indicating he was either writer or stylist or both. Music and prophesy were closely linked in these leaders (1 Chronicles 25:1-2; 2 Chronicles 20:14-23 and 29:30).

1 Chronicles 25 details the Levites who directed three family choirs or guilds and served as temple singers:

> David, together with the commanders of the army, set apart some of the sons of Asaph, Heman, and Juduthun for the

> ministry of prophesying, accompanied by harps, lyres and
> cymbals . . . for the ministry at the house of God. Asaph,
> Juduthun and Heman were under the supervision of the king.
> Along with their relatives—all of them trained and skilled in
> music for the Lord—they numbered 288 (1 Chronicles 25:1,
> 6-7, *NIV*).

Given the centrality of the Psalms to Old and New Testament
worship, the importance of the choristers is establishing the literature and atmosphere of celebration is obvious. In today's church,
music and celebration can still model a prophetic and climate-
setting stance.

The sages tutored and advised the kings. They were the
consultants or "owls"[1] of their day who provided an intellectual
dimension for leadership. The sages generally served in behind-
the-scenes staff roles but were frequently the powers behind the
throne. Because they were in influential positions, they often
adopted a low-key, low-risk, "keep us in office" attitude. These
intellectuals, a professional class to themselves, were pragmatic,
conservative, and international in outlook. Solomon's wisdom
became the prototype for the sages.

The sages contributed the materials that have become the
advice columns of the Bible. The perspectives and flavor of
wisdom are found in the Proverbs, Daniel, Ecclesiastes as well as
in John 1:1-18 and Colossians 1. The insights of wisdom literature
are basic in understanding Christology, the study of what the
Ultimate Leader did and who He was.

Each of us needs persons we choose to "be like." While some
of our models are famous, the vast majority of our heroines and
heroes are those leaders whose claim to fame is steadiness. They
were consistent and available, or, as Woody Allen has said of
successful people, they "showed up eighty percent of the time!"

Model Building

Charles Sheldon's classic religious novel, In His Steps, *raised a modeling question that's still relevant for leaders: What would Jesus do? Such a basic model stabilizes leaders because it zeroes in on the "be like" issue. Consider these illustrations of modeling.*

Her choir members called her a "gentle general."[2] For more than 2,000 Sundays over forty-one years, Geraldine Cate directed her church's choir. She planned and led worship with one pastor for twenty-five years. His description of Gerry Cate? "Even though she's something of a saint, saints can be trying. She has perseverance, pushiness, bravado . . . She believed so much in what she was doing that she was dogged, she was tenacious." Her current pastor sees Gerry as "a living symbol of continuity" across many significant changes in her church. Free private lessons were available to choir members, a service Gerry Cate considered part of her role as minister of music. A choir member of thirty years depicts Gerry Cate as a model: "You just don't let her down, because she doesn't let us down." Do you want to "be like" Gerry Cate and model her unswerving constancy?

He's now chairman of a Wall Street investment firm. Even though it's been almost half a century since she taught him at Broughton High School in Raleigh, North Carolina, Richard Jenrette swears that he still hears Miss Mary Sue Fonville's voice every time he stands up to make a speech: "Outline and keep it logical."[3] Miss Fonville, he remembers, "taught us to outline. She taught logic. She cleared so many cobwebs out of my mind I'm eternally grateful." So grateful in fact that Jenrette gave $100,000 to endow awards for today's excellent teachers. Do you want to "be like" Miss Mary Sue Fonville and imprint basic ideas on others' minds? Or, do you want to "be like" Richard Jenrette and reflect your sages' values and generosity?

Some social commentators sadly observe that we now live in an age without heroes or heroines. If true, that's a new perspective. In the past, we've lionized warriors, saints, Renaissance men, frontiersmen and cowboys, rags-to-riches tycoons, and sports figures. But these social commentators suggest the last true American hero passed off the scene when the final vestiges of the western frontier were tamed. Now, we are left only with celebrities.

Psychologist Carl Jung viewed heroes from various cultures and observed that they tended to follow a common course: they left home and were tutored by a wise teacher, gained fame, struggled against evil and won, and sacrificed for their causes— potentially at the cost of their lives. Surely every culture has teachers, rights activists, astronauts, athletes, political figures, and ministers who move us to commit to causes and help us conquer our darker instincts. It's up to us to provide models and mentors for tomorrow's leaders.

Searching for Healthy Models

Wanted: Leaders who recognize the importance of positive models and seek them out in order to learn from them.

Wanted: Leaders who learn from a variety of models—holy persons, celebrants, and consultants.

Wanted: Leaders who choose models, whether they are famous or obscure.

Wanted: Leaders who are willing to serve as models and mentors for the next generation of leaders.

* * * * *

The Bell Tolls for You

The great leaders we've surveyed in this book have plenty of good news for contemporary leaders. These leaders demonstrate that effective leaders are self-aware, other-sensitive, and situation-wise. As self-aware, leaders know who they are and exercise their influence maturely. As other-sensitive, leaders care about their followers and intend to develop them for responsible future leadership opportunities. As situation-wise, leaders read the demands of settings and systems well and work strategically in these circumstances. These three ingredients of great leadership set the target high. With expectations so lofty, we must choose to be leaders with care and act reflectively.

Will Campbell in *Brother to a Dragonfly* tells a cautionary tale about his grandfather's view of leadership. Will, his brother Joe, and their grandfather, according to the story, were looking for their livestock in their Mississippi pasture land. Their search was guided by the distant sound of a cow bell. The old man noted that the cow to be belled had to be chosen with care. Why? Because the rest of the herd followed that belled cow! So a rover or a fighter or a fence breaker made a risky leader. The grandfather offered these observations on leadership in the animal world without interpretation or application.

But Will and Joe knew what their grandfather's little parable implied for youngsters—and oldsters. Will comments that "if we couldn't become leaders we would have no choice but to follow someone else's bell."[1]

Wear the bell and lead. Or listen for the bell and follow. Or try to track the bell and become part of the situation. There are your options. The sound of the bells calls us to leadership. Our challenge? Act with the vision and compassion of the Bible's great leaders.

DISCUSSION GUIDE

The following suggestions for discussion are intended for a classroom study series or a training retreat or conference. Choose the themes you want to emphasize or explore, and use the questions and models below to stimulate discussion.

To prepare for each discussion, read some quality Bible commentaries, Old and New Testament histories, and other theological materials to deepen your understanding of the episode under consideration. Review the book's information on each episode. Then use the items below to help your group make leadership applications.

Introduction

1. How do you know a leader when you see one? How do leaders act? What do they do?

2. God, like all effective leaders, acts. Theologians typically describe God's actions as Creator, Judge, and Redeemer. Can you identify biblical episodes of God's leadership initiatives in these three areas?

3. Post the formal definition, "Leadership is an action-oriented, interpersonal influencing process," and challenge your group to modify it. For example, a simple definition of a leader is "one with followers."

4. As an orientation aid for the remainder of your discussions, draw a triangle and label the apex "Leader's Style" and the two base points "Followers' Style" and "Situational Demands." Ask your group mem-

bers to consider these elements as basic to most leadership events and to be alert to the interaction of these ingredients as they read the episodes in *Good News from Great Leaders.*

Chapter 1

1. How did the kingdom of God vision motivate Jesus?

2. How are effective leaders "dream merchants?" What constitutes a leadership vision, and how is it developed?

3. What relationship do you see between leadership and lordship?

4. If leaders are "transformers," whom and what do they transform?

Chapter 2

1. Mordecai was identified simply as "the Jew." If you were personally limited to a two-word identifier—other than your name—what two words would you select? Why?

2. Malcolm Muggeridge, one-time agnostic turned Christian, made a strong self-defining statement: "As far as I am concerned, it is Christ or nothing."[1] Can you think of biblical incidents that contain the same kind of statements?

3. Self-defining leaders (1) say "I" (2) in the group context of "we" (3) while taking clear positions and (4) keeping cool. Which of these four steps do you find most difficult? How do you cope with this difficulty?

4. Use the model on the following page to help your group members sharpen their sense of selfhood for leadership.

BE/BELIEVE/BEHAVE

Clarifying Personal Identity

Jesus instructed us to let "yes" clearly mean "yes" and "no" simply mean "no" (Matthew 5:37). What we say yes and no to defines and identifies us. If so, "yes = me" and "no = not me."

Who we are and what we believe is demonstrated every day in how we behave. Below you'll see several arenas of identity. In each category, please complete the "yes" and "no" statements.

IDENTITY ARENAS	Yes, I AM . . . !!!	No, I AM NOT. . .!!!
abilities/skills		
traits/qualities		
family/friends/ relationships		
beliefs/values/ commitments		
achievements/ recognition/ affirmations		

Chapter 3

1. God made a covenant with Abraham in Genesis 12:1-3, promising land, ancestry, and blessing. Some commentators feel the central question of the patriarchal stories is, "Can (and will) God keep his promises?" How did God prove his integrity in these stories?

2. Was General Dean right? If we lose our integrity, have we lost everything?

3. What are the major shortcuts today's leaders are most frequently tempted to take?

Chapter 4

1. What basic lessons did Jacob learn from experience?

2. Is success or failure the better teacher?

3. How can trial-and-error be transformed into trial-and-success?

4. Apply Blanchard and Peale's three "ethical check" questions to a crucial decision you or your group is facing.

Chapter 5

1. What does Ezekiel's call for more follower-oriented leaders say to contemporary leaders?

2. Are leaders or followers more important to an enterprise?

3. Would you prefer to follow a king, prophet, warrior, or shepherd? Why?

4. Is Stayer's "The Question Is the Answer" plaque a practical leadership approach?

Chapter 6

1. Considering Paul's life in its broader New Testament context, what do you suppose the "this one thing I do" was that he mentioned?

2. How can leaders, like Paul, make use of the debit sides of their life ledgers while staying more focused on their credit experiences?

3. If you had 30 seconds to give a "stump speech" about the focus in your life, what would you say? Why?

Chapter 7

1. Identify some *kairos* events in the Bible. How do these situations differ from merely chronological circumstances?

2. Post the four-style leadership model below as a visual aid for exploring Jesus' application of leadership styles. Identify instances in which Jesus used each style.

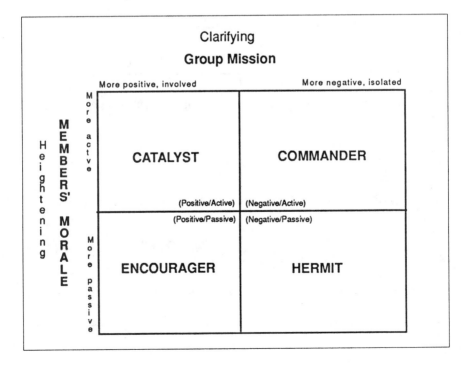

3. Identify a situation in which you used a less appropriate and less effective leader style than was apparently called for. How was your style out-of-sync? How did you know a different style would have worked better? Which style would have fit more aptly? Do you now see your style-flex options more clearly?

Chapter 8

1. Nehemiah has been called the first city manager. How did he deal with people and projects in ways that might allow him to function effectively as a contemporary civic leader?

2. Kouzes and Posner's five leadership practices reflect both sides— mission and morale—of organizational effectiveness. Two of the practices relate to mission and the other two to morale. The fifth practice is embodied in the leader and links mission and morale together. Use the model below to depict the relationship among the five practices and the mission-morale mix.

MISSION	MORALE
Challenging the Process	**Enabling** Others to Act
and	and
Inspiring a Shared Vision	**Encouraging** the Heart
Modeling the Way	

3. Why is the mission-morale balance difficult to maintain?

4. Below is a summary handout on Kouzes and Posner's leadership practices. These five actions are arranged on a spectrum with the two more mission-oriented practices toward the left margin and the two more morale-oriented practices toward the right margin. Additionally, ten specific actions are noted for leaders to use in daily leadership activities. How can these practices be applied in daily leadership opportunities?

A Spectrum of Leadership Practice

MISSION ^
|
|
|
|
|
|
|
|
|
|
MORALE v

I. Inspiring a Shared Vision
   1. Envision an Uplifting and Ennobling Future.
   2. Enlist Others in a Common Vision by Appealing to their Values, Interests, Hopes, and Dreams.

II. Challenging the Process
   3. Search Out Challenging Opportunities to Change, Grow, Innovate, and Improve.
   4. Experiment, Take Risks, and Learn from the Accompanying Mistakes.

III. Modeling the Way
   5. Set the Example for Others by Behaving in Ways That are Consistent with Your Shared Values.
   6. Plan Small Wins That Promote Consistent Progress and Build Commitment.

IV. Enabling Others to Act
   7. Foster Collaboration by Promoting Cooperative Goals and Building Trust.
   8. Strengthen People by Sharing Information and Power and Increasing Their Discretion and Visibility.

V. Encouraging the Heart
   9. Recognize Individual Contributions to the Success of Every Project.
   10. Celebrate Team Accomplishments Regularly.

Chapter 9

1. Contrast boss-ship and leadership.

2. Why is directive leadership needed in unstable and overstable situations?

3. What happens when Commanders try to lead during stable eras or with mature followers?

4. Why does boss-ship tend to be limited to only a generation or two? (The comfort of followers' dependence for both leaders and followers as well as the tendency of powerless persons to resist, rebel, and turn the tables on persons who "one-up" them are likely observations from your group members.)

5. How could leaders create crises and abuse their stewardship of power?

Chapter 10

1. Study the five New Testament stories about Barnabas, the Encourager. What kinds of encouraging leader actions do these incidents specify?

2. When did you know that you deserved blame, but someone gave you the benefit of the doubt? How did you feel? What did you learn from the experience?

3. Who are the "organizational priests" in your workplace? In your study group? How do they act? Why are they important to group health?

Chapter 11

1. What would the Hebrew childrens' "organizational chart" look like before the pivotal episode in Exodus 18? (Moses' name would appear in

every box of the chart.) Draw the chart for impact, and post it for group discussion.

2. Post and discuss this challenge statement: "There is one best leader style for all circumstances! One size fits all leadership situations!"

3. What are some signals you read when you're using a leader style that's too heavy-handed or too over-responsible?

4. Why are consultants akin to Jethro helpful to leaders?

Chapter 12

1. When you read Mark 10:35-45, did you identify more with James and John or the remaining ten apostles? Why?

2. How can a boss still function as a servant? (Is there a clue in the "cause and community" focus of Jesus?)

3. Distinguish between a leader stance and a leader style.

4. How can a contemporary leader follow Mosley's suggestion and "lead with a towel?"

Chapter 13

1. If strategy is "the art of devising and employing plans toward a goal," what was Paul's primary goal in Acts?

2. Imagine Paul as a marketer or advertiser. How would he have approached the five strategic actions we've noted?

3. Discuss the contrasts between strategic thinkers and risk-free actors. Which would you rather be?

4. As a broader Bible study option on strategic thinking, use the handout on the following page to view the entire book of Acts as mission strategy.

Acts As Mission Strategy:
Examining the Panels of Acts for Strategy Pointers

Empowering Strategies (Acts 1:1-6:7)

Begin where you are geographically (1:1-8)
Rely on God's Spirit (1:9-2:13)
Preach what you know (2:14-47)
Use resistance to toughen resolve (3:1-5:42)
Organize for ministry (6:1-7)

Diversifying Strategies (Acts 6:8-9:31)

Count the cost of bold missions (6:8-8:3)
Let the Gospel confront your prejudices (8:4-40)
Enlist leaders for future work (9:1-31)

Anticipating Strategies (Acts 9:32-12:25)

Recognize new fields of service (9:32-11:18)
Avoid a superstar attitude (11:19-26)
Allow adversity to build fellowship (11:27-12:25)

Launching Strategies (Acts 13:1-16:5)

Use base camps as launch pads (13:1-3)
Appeal to the half-converts (13:4-41)
Respond to the responsive groups. (13:42-14:28)
Declare doctrine clearly (15:1-35)
Stabilize new believers (15:36-16:5)

Expanding Strategies (Acts 16:6-19:20)

Take advantage of new openings (16:6-10)
Visit strategic sites, win groups, and train them for mission
     (16:11-19:20)
Communicate in the audience's thought forms (17:16-34)

Planning Strategies (Acts 19:21-28:31)

Set a goal and act on it (19:21-21:26)
Exercise patience and persistence (21:27-28:16)
Endure rejection for a free Gospel (28:17-31)

Chapter 14

1. How were you taught to view anger as a religious issue?

2. Why do feelings become confused with the facts in conflict situations?

3. How can Fisher and Ury's four principles be applied to conflict situations?

4. How do you decide when to turn the other cheek and when to turn the tables?

Chapter 15

1. What modern "wide open" city reminds you of Corinth? Why?

2. Think of a factional group you once belonged to. Why did you join? What "advantages" accrued to you for belonging? Why did you move away from that faction?

3. Post and discuss this challenge statement: "Differences enrich group life."

4. When were you "triangled" recently? Use Friedman's "seven laws" to analyze your triangle.

Chapter 16

1. If you were Saul, how would you want David to relate to you? If you were David, how would you want Saul to relate to you?

2. Describe the most difficult boss you've ever known. What made the situation especially uncomfortable?

3. Illustrate this theme: "Any ability—when overused—can become a liability."

4. Review David's six actions toward the unbalanced Saul. What else could he have done?

5. Maybe there were good reasons Saul was such an inept supervisor. (1) He was inexperienced as any "first" leader is apt to be. After all, he moved from herdsman to king with a very short resume. (2) He worked in an unstable organization, a not-yet nation. (3) He felt abandoned, isolated, and without quality relationships. (4) He blamed others for his problems. Do these reasons "forgive" Saul?

Chapter 17

1. What are the unique risks in dramatic victories like Elijah experienced on Mount Carmel?

2. Contrast success and failure.

3. How do the four features of the "Elijah trap" open the door to depression? How can those ingredients of discouragement be resisted?

4. How can "self-talk" influence our moods?

Chapter 18

1. When you think of the twelve apostles, whom do you think of first? Whom do you overlook? What do your memory preferences suggest about your leadership approach?

2. If the "V" formation geese use in flight makes them more efficient flyers, where do you see similar teamwork typically practiced?

3. Evaluate your work group or study group against the eight reasons team building is generally needed.

Chapter 19

1. The biblical world was patriarchal. How are the norms of a culture, an organization, or a congregation changed to make leadership more gender inclusive?

2. How do you feel about the research that shows women are better planners than men?

3. Where do you observe the most obvious examples of the "glass ceiling"?

Chapter 20

1. List the most attractive biblical models for leadership. Did you include groups as well as individuals?

2. Did you relate more naturally to the traditionalism of the Nazarites, the climate setting of the choristers, or the tutoring of the sages? Why?

3. How do your models or mentors shape your leadership approach? How can you become an effective model for future leaders?

4. Is our age without heroes and heroines?

NOTES

Introduction

    1. Alden Thompson, "God's Word: Casebook or Codebook?" *Ministry* (July 1991), 6-10.
    2. G. Ernest Wright, *God Who Acts: Biblical Theology as Recital,* Studies in Biblical Theology, No. 8 (London: SCM Press, 1952).
    3. Lawrence Toombs, *Nation Making*, Bible Guides, No. 4 (Nashville: Abingdon Press, 1962), 35.
    4. James McCribben, *Leadership: Strategies for Organizational Effectiveness* (New York: AMACOM, 1981), v.

Chapter 1

    1. James McGregor Burns, *Leadership* (New York: Harper & Row, 1978).
    2. Ibid, 20.

Chapter 2

    1. Edwin H. Friedman, *Generation to Generation: Family Process in Church and Synagogue* (New York: Guilford Press, 1985), 220-249.
    2. Ibid, 27.

Chapter 3

1. Joseph L. Badaracco, Jr. and Richard R. Ellsworth, *Leadership and the Quest for Integrity* (Boston: Harvard Business School Press, 1989).
2. Max DePree, *Leadership Is an Art* (New York: Dell, 1989), 85.

Chapter 4

1. Kenneth Blanchard and Norman Vincent Peale, *The Power of Ethical Management* (New York: William Morrow, 1988).

Chapter 5

1. John Haggai, "The Search for the Good Shepherd," *Ministries Today* (May-June, 1990), 81.
2. Trudy Heller and Jon Van Til, "Leadership and Followership: Some Summary Propositions," *Journal of Applied Behavioral Science* (1982, Vol. 18, No. 3), 407.
3. Ronald Lippit, "The Changing Leader-Follower Relationships of the 1980s," *Journal of Applied Behavioral Science* (1982, Vol. 18, No. 3), 397.
4. Ralph Stayer, "How I Learned to Let My Workers Lead," *Harvard Business Review* (November-December, 1990), 83.
5. Ibid, 75 and 80.

Chapter 6

1. Tom Peters, *Thriving on Chaos: Handbook for a Management Revolution* (New York: Alfred A. Knopf, 1988), 406-407.

Chapter 7

1. Robert D. Dale, *Pastoral Leadership* (Nashville: Abingdon Press, 1986), 39-53.

2. Ron Zemke, "Better Ways to Help Train People," *Training/ HRD* (August 1976), 12-16.

Chapter 8

1. Ernest E. Mosley, "Nehemiah: Builder of Walls and People" in *Leadership Profiles from Bible Personalities* (Nashville: Broadman Press, 1979), 62-85.
2. James M. Kouzes and Barry Z. Posner, *The Leadership Challenge: How to Get Extraordinary Things Done in Organizations* (San Francisco: Jossey-Bass Publishers, 1989).

Chapter 9

1. Robert D. Dale, *Pastoral Leadership* (Nashville: Abingdon Press, 1986), 42-44 and 69-71.
2. Wess Roberts, *Leadership Secrets of Attila the Hun* (New York: Warner Communications, 1985), 26.
3. Ibid, 47.
4. Ibid, 46.
5. James MacGregor Burns, *Leadership* (New York: Harper & Row, 1978), 18.

Chapter 10

1. Robert D. Dale, *Pastoral Leadership* (Nashville: Abingdon Press, 1986), 44-45 and 71-74.
2. Terrence E. Deal and Allan A. Kennedy, *Corporate Cultures: The Rites and Rituals of Corporate Life* (Reading, MA: Addison-Wesley Publishing, 1982), 52-53.
3. Ibid, 88-90.

Chapter 11

1. Robert D. Dale, *Pastoral Leadership* (Nashville: Abingdon Press, 1986), 42-44.

2. Daniel Tagliere, *People, Power, and Organization* (New York: AMACOM, 1973), 12.

Chapter 12

1. Robert K. Greenleaf, *Servant Leadership* (New York: Paulist Press, 1977).

Chapter 13

1. I consider myself lucky to work daily with one of the best strategic planners in religious life today, Reggie McDonough. Although I can't document specifics, I'm sure many of the practical ideas in this section are principles I've learned from Reggie by osmosis.

Chapter 14

1. Roger Fisher and William Ury, *Getting to Yes* (Boston: Houghton Mifflin, 1981).
2. C.S. Lewis, *Mere Christianity* (New York: Macmillan Company, 1943), 174.
3. Helmut Thielicke, *How the World Began* (Philadelphia: Fortress Press, 1961), 134.

Chapter 15

1. Edwin H. Friedman, *Generation to Generation* (New York: Guilford Press, 1985), 36-39.

Chapter 16

1. Mardy Grothe and Peter Wylie, *Problem Bosses* (New York: Facts on File Publications, 1987).
2. Laurence J. Peter, *The Peter Principle* (New York: William Morrow, 1969).

3. Grothe and Wylie, *Problem Bosses*, 8.

4. Robert E. Kaplan, "The Expansive Executive," *Issues and Observations*, (Vol. 10, No. 4), 1-6.

Chapter 17

1. Martin E.P. Seligman, *Learned Optimism* (New York: Alfred A. Knopf, 1991), 203-204.

Chapter 18

1. Robert D. Dale, "Leadership-Followership: the Church's Challenge," *Southwestern Journal of Theology*, (Vol. 29, No. 2), 23-28.

2. Max DePree, *Leadership Is an Art* (New York: Dell Publishing, 1989), 25-26.

Chapter 19

1. Jennifer Juergens, "Take That, Buster!" *Successful Meetings*, June 1991, 47-48, 50.

2. Marilyn Loden, *Feminine Leadership* (New York: Time Books, 1985). An additional helpful perspective on female dimensions of leadership is Judy B. Rosener's "Ways Women Lead," *Harvard Business Review*, (November-December, 1990), 119-125.

Chapter 20

1. James L. Lowery, Jr., *Peers, Tents, and Owls* (New York: Morehouse-Barlow Company, 1973).

2. Melanie Sill, "'Ms. Pullen Memorial' Hangs up Her Choir Director's Robe," *News and Observer*, (Raleigh, NC, April 28, 1985), p. 1C.

3. Holly Selby, "Teachers Who Made a Difference," *The Raleigh Times*, (NC, May 17, 1985), p. 1B.

Conclusion

1. Will D. Campbell, *Brother to a Dragonfly* (New York: Continuum Publishing, 1977), 26.

Discussion Guide

1. Malcolm Muggeridge, *Jesus Rediscovered* (Wheaton, IL: Tyndale House Publishers, 1969), 58.

SELECTED BIBLIOGRAPHY ON RELIGIOUS LEADERSHIP

Badaracco, Joseph L. Jr. and Ellsworth, Richard R. *Leadership and the Quest for Integrity.* Boston: Harvard Business School Press, 1989.

Barber, James David. *The Presidential Character: Predicting Performance in the White House.* Englewood Cliffs, NJ: Prentice-Hall, 1972.

Bennis, Warren and Nanus, Bert. *Leaders: the Strategies for Taking Charge.* New York: Harper and Row, 1985.

Bernstein, Paula. *Family Ties, Corporate Bonds.* Garden City, NY: Doubleday, 1985.

Bierstedt, Robert. *The Social Order.* New York: McGraw-Hill, 1974.

Bratcher, Edward B. *The Walk-on-Water Syndrome.* Waco, TX: Word Books, 1984.

Burns, James McGregor. *Leadership.* New York: Harper and Row, 1978.

Callahan, Kennon L. *Effective Church Leadership: Building on the Twelve Keys.* New York: Harper and Row, 1990.

Carroll, Jackson W., Dudley, Carl S., and McKinney, William, editors. *Handbook of Congregational Studies.* Nashville: Abingdon, 1986.

Clinton, J. Robert. *The Making of a Leader: Recognizing the Lessons and Stages of Leadership Development.* Colorado Springs: Navpress, 1989.

Connor, Patrick E. and Lake, Linda K. *Managing Organizational Change.* New York: Praeger, 1988.

Dale, Robert D. *Keeping the Dream Alive: Understanding and Building Congregational Morale.* Nashville: Broadman Press, 1988.

___. *Ministers as Leaders.* Nashville: Broadman Press, 1984.

___. *Pastoral Leadership: a Handbook of Resources for Congregational Leadership.* Nashville: Abingdon Press, 1986.

___. *Surviving Difficult Church Members.* Nashville: Abingdon, 1984.

___. *To Dream Again: How to Help Your Church Come Alive.* Nashville: Broadman Press, 1981.

Davis, Anne and Rowatt, Wade Jr., editors. *Formation for Christian Ministry.* Louisville, KY: Review and Expositor, 1981.

Deal, Terrence E. and Kennedy, Allan A. *Corporate Cultures: the Rites and Rituals of Corporate Life.* Reading, MA: Addison-Wesley, 1982.

DePree, Max. *Leadership Is an Art.* New York: Doubleday, 1989.

DeVries, Manfred F.R. and Miller, Danny. *The Neurotic Organizatrion.* San Francisco: Jossey-Bass, 1984.

Frances, Allen. Audiotapes. *DSM-III Personality Disorders: Diagnosis and Treatment.* New York: Guilford, 1988.

Friedman, Edwin H. *Generation to Generation: Family Process in Church and Synagogue.* New York: Guilford Press, 1985.

Greenleaf, Robert K. *Servant Leadership: a Journey into the Nature of Legitimate Power and Greatness.* New York: Paulist Press, 1977.

Hart, Archibald D. *Coping with Depression in the Ministry and Other Helping Professions.* Waco, TX: Word Books, 1984.

Keirsey, David and Bates, Marilyn. *Please Understand Me: Character and Temperament Types.* Del Mar, CA: Prometheus Nemesis Book Company, 1984.

Kliewer, Stephen. *How to Live with Diversity in the Local Church.* Washington, DC: Alban Institute, 1987.

Kouzes, James M. and Posner, Barry Z. *The Leadership Challenge: How to Get Extraordinary Things Done in Organizations.* San Francisco: Jossey-Bass Publishers, 1989.

Kroeger, Otto and Thuesen, Janet M. *Type Talk: or How to Determine Your Personality Type and Change Your Life.* New York: Delecorte Press, 1988.

Kuhne, Gary W. *The Change Factor: the Risks and Joys.* Grand Rapids, MI: Zondervan, 1986.

Leavitt, Harold J. *Corporate Pathfinders: Building Vision and Values into Organizations.* Homewood, IL: Dow-Jones-Irwin, 1986.

Levinson, Daniel J. *The Seasons of a Man's Life.* New York: Knopf, 1978.

Lippitt, Gordon L. *Visualizing Change: Model Building and the Change Process.* Fairfax, VA: NTL Learning Resources, 1973.

Maloney, Mercedes Lynch and Maloney, Anne. *The Hand That Rocks the Cradle: Mothers, Sons, and Leadership.* Englewood Cliffs, NJ: Prentice-Hall, 1985.

McAdams, Dan P. *Power, Intimacy, and the Life Story: Psychological Inquiries into Identity.* New York: Guilford Press, 1988.

McBurney, Louis. *Every Pastor Needs a Pastor.* Waco, TX: Word Books, 1977.

McConkey, Dale D. *MBO for Nonprofit Organizations.* New York: AMACOM, 1975.

Means, James E. *Leadership in Christian Ministry.* New York: Doubleday, 1989.

Millon, Theodore. *Disorders of Personality, DSM-III: Axis II.* New York: Wiley-Interscience, 1981.

Moreman, William M. *Developing Spiritually and Professionally.* Philadelphia: Westminster, 1984.

Mosley, Ernest E. *Called to Joy: a Design for Pastoral Ministries*. Nashville: Convention Press, 1973.

___. *Leadership Profiles from Bible Personalities*. Nashville: Broadman Press, 1979.

___. *Priorities in Ministry*. Nashville: Convention Press, 1978.

Oates, Wayne E. *Behind the Masks: Personality Disorders in Religious Behavior*. Philadelphia: Westminster, 1987.

Odiorne, George S. *The Change Resisters: How They Prevent Progress and What Managers Can Do about Them*. Englewood Cliffs, NJ: Prentice-Hall, 1981.

Oldham, John M. and Morris, Lois B. *The Personality Self-Portrait*. New York: Bantam, 1990.

Oswald, Roy M. and Kroeger, Otto. *Personality Type and Religious Leadership*. Washington, DC: The Alban Institute, 1988.

Pattison, E. Mansell. *Pastor and Parish—a Systems Approach*. Philadelphia: Fortress Press, 1977.

Peters, Tom. *Thriving on Chaos: Handbook for a Management Revolution*. New York: Alfred A. Knopf, 1988.

Riggio, Ronald E. *The Charisma Quotient: What It Is, How to Get It, How to Use It*. New York: Dodd, Mead and Company, 1987.

Sanford, John A. *The Man Who Wrestled with God: Light from the Old Testament on the Psychology of Individuation*. New York: Paulist Press, 1987.

Schaller, Lyle E. *Getting Things Done: Concepts and Skills for Leaders*. Nashville: Abingdon Press, 1986.

___. *Hey, That's Our Church!* Nashville: Abingdon, 1975.

Sheehy, Gail. *Passages: Predictable Crises of Adult Life*. New York: E.P. Dutton, 1976.

Somerville, Charles. *Leadership Strategies for Ministers*. Philadelphia: Westminster Press, 1987.

Stone, Elizabeth. *Black Sheep and Kissing Cousins: How Our Family Stories Shape Us*. New York: Times Books, 1988.

Walrath, Douglas Alan. *Frameworks: Patterns for Living and Believing Today.* New York: Pilgrim Press, 1987.

White, John. *Excellence in Leadership: Reaching Goals with Prayer, Courage and Determination.* Downers Grove, IL: InterVarsity Press, 1986.

Youssef, Michael. *The Leadership Style of Jesus: How to Develop the Leadership Qualities of the Good Shepherd.* Wheaton, IL: Victor Books, 1986.

The Alban Institute:
an invitation to membership

The Alban Institute, begun in 1979, believes that the congregation is essential to the task of equipping the people of God to minister in the church and the world. A multi-denominational membership organization, the Institute provides on-site training, educational programs, consulting, research, and publishing for hundreds of churches across the country.

The Alban Institute invites you to be a member of this partnership of laity, clergy, and executives—a partnership that brings together people who are raising important questions about congregational life and people who are trying new solutions, making new discoveries, finding a new way of getting clear about the task of ministry. The Institute exists to provide you with the kinds of information and resources you need to support your ministries.

Join us now and enjoy these benefits:

Action Information, a highly respected journal published six times a year, to keep you up to date on current issues and trends.

Inside Information, Alban's quarterly newsletter, keeps you informed about research and other happenings around Alban. Available to members only.

Publications Discounts:

☐ 15% for Individual, Retired Clergy, and Seminarian Members
☐ 25% for Congregational Members
☐ 40% for Judicatory and Seminary Executive Members

Discounts on Training and Education Events

Write our Membership Department at the address below or call us at (202) 244-7320 for more information about how to join The Alban Institute's growing membership, particularly about Congregational Membership in which 12 designated persons receive all benefits of membership.

The Alban Institute, Inc.
4125 Nebraska Avenue, NW
Washington, DC 20016